joy
OF SCRAPBOOKING
by Lisa Bearnson

completely
revised and
expanded

A LEISURE ARTS PUBLICATION

Managing Editor SUSAN WHITE SULLIVAN

Special Projects Director SUSAN FRANTZ WILES

Director of Designer Relations DEBRA NETTLES

Senior Prepress Director MARK HAWKINS

Publishing Systems Administrator BECKY RIDDLE

Publishing Systems Assistants CLINT HANSON, JOHN ROSE,
KEIJI YUMOTO, AND CARRIE EAST

Vice President and Chief Operating Officer TOM SIEBENMORGEN

Director of Corporate Planning and Development LATICIA MULL DITTRICH

Vice President, Sales and Marketing PAM STEBBINS

Director of Sales and Services MARGARET REINOLD

Vice President, Operations JIM DITTRICH

Comptroller, Operations ROB THIEME

Retail Customer Service Manager STAN RAYNOR

Print Production Manager FRED F. PRUSS

creating Keepsakes

Founding Editor   LISA BEARNSON

Editor-In-Chief   BRIAN TIPPETTS

Creative Editor   BRITNEY MELLEN

Senior Writer   RACHEL THOMAE

Project Manager/Contributing Writer   DENISE PAULEY

Senior Editor   VANESSA HOY

Copy Editor   KIM SANDOVAL

Editorial Assistants   JOANNIE McBRIDE, FRED BREWER

Project Coordinator   LIESL RUSSELL

Art Director, Special Projects   ERIN BAYLESS

Senior Designer, Special Projects   NATALIE REICH

Photography   AMERICAN COLOR

CK MEDIA

Chief Executive Officer   DAVID O'NEIL

Chief Marketing Officer   ANDREW JOHNSON

Controller   SCOTT FAMBROUGH

VP/Editorial Director   LIN SORENSON

VP/Consumer Marketing   SUSAN DuBOIS

VP/Director of Events   PAULA KRAEMER

VP/Group Publisher   TINA BATTOCK

VP/Online Director   CHAD PHELPS

Senior Production Director   TERRY BOYER

Library of Congress Control Number: 2008921952

Tippetts, Brian
Creating Keepsakes
"A Leisure Arts Publication"

ISBN-13: 978-1-60140-841-9
ISBN-10: 1-60140-841-2

contents

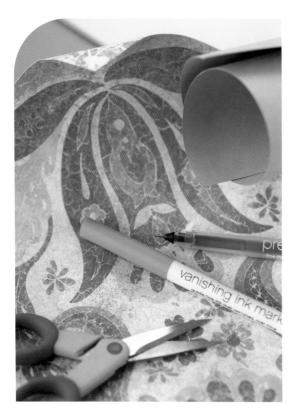

scrapbooking from a-z

IN 1998, *CREATING KEEPSAKES* PUBLISHED its very first book—*Joy of Scrapbooking*. It was a dream come true for me and my staff. An avid scrapbooker, I was thrilled that we'd had the chance to publish an encyclopedic volume that covered everything from A to Z about scrapbooking. It was a valuable resource for all scrapbookers: a book that would help guide them through the world of photo-safe scrapbooking, a book that would give readers lots of inspirational ideas and answer all of their questions about getting started.

As I look back at our first book, I realize that our overall message about scrapbooking remains the same as it did 10 years ago. Scrapbooking is *still* a wonderful way to preserve family memories in a creative and fulfilling way. And while I'll admit that styles and techniques have greatly changed (I no longer cut my photos into stars and balloons!), the joy of scrapbooking remains the same. What's not to love about creating layouts that future generations will cherish?

Scrapbooking has grown by leaps and bounds in the last 10 years, and that's why we decided to revise and update our original book. In this new edition, you'll find all the updated information you'll need to get started scrapbooking today or to welcome a friend or family member into this hobby. This book is also a wonderful resource for the experienced scrapbooker—it's filled with hundreds of inspirational ideas, brand-new page layouts, artistic techniques and more.

Ten years ago, I invited readers of our first book to join me in scrapbooking their memories in a way that's both safe and enjoyable. Today, I invite you to do the same.

Ready to get started? Let's go!

Lisa Bearnson

Handwritten journaling around photo: This I know for sure ... children - not possessions, not position, not prestige - are my greatest treasures. I am a nurturer. I am a teacher. I am a protector. I am a leader. I am strong and immovable. I will not give up during disappointment or difficulty.

my simple truth

MY SIMPLE TRUTH by Lisa Bearnson. **Supplies** *Cardstock:* Bazzill Basics Paper; *Rub-on flower:* American Crafts; *Letter die cuts:* Cricut, Provo Craft; *Pen:* Slick Writer, American Crafts.

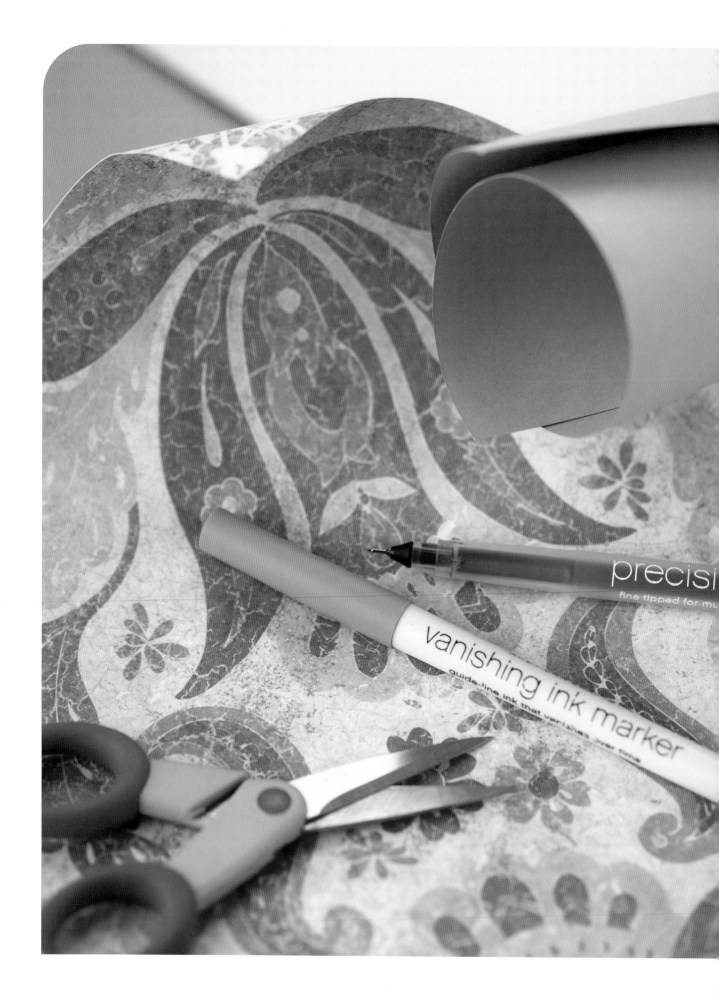

precisi

fine tipped for mu

vanishing ink marker

guide-line ink that vanishes over time

basics

I put my first scrapbook together when I was seven years old—a huge album filled with school pictures and projects. Unfortunately, I created this keepsake with tape, construction paper, rubber cement and felt-tip pens . . . and it's now faded and falling apart. Luckily, today's archival products prevent that from happening. Here's a rundown of the supplies you'll want to buy, along with tips I wish I'd had when I started scrapbooking. And for a closer look at some of these supplies, turn to Chapter 6!

SCRAPBOOK ESSENTIALS

Although shopping for scrap-booking supplies may seem like a daunting (but definitely *fun*) task, it's actually quite simple if you stick to the basics. You'll only need a handful of items to design your first layout. Start with those, then add to your stash as you learn what you'll *really* use. For a more in-depth look at these supplies, refer to Chapter 6.

cardstock and patterned paper

The foundation of nearly every layout, cardstock comes in a variety of colors, textures and weights. It can provide a background for your page, serve as a sturdy photo mat, or be folded, texturized, stamped or torn to become an eye-catching accent. If you're just starting out, consider a selection of neutral colors like white, oatmeal and black.

Do you prefer cute or cool, pretty or funky, subtle or bold? You'll easily find patterned paper to play along with that feel. Pick patterns that complement your photos as subtle backgrounds, coordinated mats or embellishments.

pens and pencils

To start, you'll need an archival-quality, fine-tipped black marker for labels, captions, hand-drawn titles, doodles and journaling. You'll need to experiment with different pens to see which you're most comfortable using.

When you're ready for a little variety, consider markers in other colors and tip styles (like calligraphy or scroll and brush if you do elaborate hand-lettering), paint or gel pens with opaque or metallic ink, colored pencils for writing or shading, and blender and embossing pens for artistic techniques.

trimmers and scissors

Whether you're cropping a photo, trimming a patterned-paper border or hand-cutting your own embellishments, you'll definitely need a tool to simplify the job. Your most basic cutting tools are craft knives, scissors and trimmers.

A craft knife is a handheld, pen-like tool with a straight or swivel blade for precision cutting. Use it with a self-healing mat, ruler or T-square for long, straight slices. A pair of scissors is a great tool for trimming ribbon, cutting paper, etc. You can also get creative with decorative-edge scissors for a variety of effects, including scallop, deckle and zigzag edges. For straight edges, paper trimmers make quick work of cropping photos and trimming sheets of cardstock and patterned paper down to size.

adhesives

You'll need something to attach photos and accents to your layouts, and that's where adhesives come in. Although the adhesive you choose must be acid free and photo safe, this supply isn't "one size fits all;" purchase different types to suit specific applications.

① PHOTO CORNERS

When you're working with older photos (or any photo or document you'd prefer not to attach permanently to your page), photo corners are your best option. These small tabs stick to your page and serve as "pockets" to hold your picture.

② GLUE STICK

The old standby gets points for ease of use—swivel it up and dab to affix photos, chipboard accents, ribbon and photos.

③ BOTTLED GLUE

From a tiny dot to a long, thin line, liquid glue is ideal for precision applications. Use a minimal amount to prevent warping and note whether the bottle says "permanent" or "repositionable."

④ ADHESIVE DOTS

Offered in various diameters and heights, pressure-sensitive dots are surprisingly strong for their size. Use them to attach small and light or heavy and bulky embellishments, to repair rips or to tack ribbon down.

⑤ ADHESIVE REMOVER

When you need to reposition a photo or accent that has become permanently adhered to your page, reach for an adhesive remover. You can use a liquid-based solution (not pictured) to carefully remove photos and accents that are glued down. Use an eraser-type adhesive remover to remove adhesive residue.

⑥ MOUNTING SQUARES

Available in roll-on dispensers or in versions with backings, you'll need to remove them one by one. These double-sided adhesive squares are great for photos and lightweight accents.

⑦ SPRAY ADHESIVE

Aerosol spray can attach sheer paper, like vellum, without showing through and provides strong, even coverage on large areas. Use only in a well-ventilated area to avoid inhaling the fumes.

⑧ PHOTO TABS

Another double-sided adhesive option, photo tabs are available in roll-on dispensers or peel-and-stick versions in boxes. These tabs are a popular option for adhering photos, papers and other lightweight accents.

⑨ TRANSPARENT ADHESIVE

Available in a variety of styles, including adhesive dots, as shown here, transparent adhesive is ideal for adhering clear materials such as vellum or transparencies without showing through.

⑩ FOAM SQUARES

Add dimension to embellishments or photos by adhering them to your layout with foam squares. This adhesive is available in a range of sizes; larger foam squares are best for adhering heavier embellishments or larger photos.

DOUBLE-SIDED TAPE
(not pictured)

Need an adhesive that's thin but strong enough to adhere accents to textured cardstock? Double-stick tape (not pictured) is manufactured in roll or roller form and in a choice of widths. Foam varieties add lift for subtle dimension.

①

② PIONEER® EXTRA STRONG EMBELLISHMENT GLUE STICK
For Most Scrapbook Decorating Surfaces
BONDS PERMANENTLY
• Acid Free
• Non-Toxic
• Child Safe
• Dries Clear
Conforms to ASTM D-4236
Net Wt. 10 Grams / .31 Oz.

③ Aleene's ORIGINAL TACKY GLUE
ALL-PURPOSE
TOUS USAGES
PARA TODO USO
2 US FL OZ (59 mL)

④ KOKUYO Dot 'n' Roller Adhesive
PERMANENT REFILLABLE 1/3in.x43ft.

⑤

⑥ Scrapbook Adhesives™ by 3L
500 CLEAR
Click 'n Stick
Mounting Squares
◇ No blue tabs
◇ Acid free/archival safe
Permanent™

⑦ perfect for VELLUM VELLUM perfect for VELLUM perfect for VELLUM perfect
creative IMAGINATIONS
Scrappers' Spray
◆ Invisible Adhesive Spray
◆ Temporarily Re-positionable
◆ Photo Safe
CREATING KEEPSAKES CK OK APPROVED PRODUCT
DANGER! EXTREMELY FLAMMABLE LIQUID AND VAPOR. VAPORS MAY CAUSE FLASH FIRE. CONTENTS UNDER PRESSURE. Read other cautions on back panel.
NET WT. 7.0 OZ (199g)

⑧ We R

⑨ 10 SHEETS   TRANSPARENT ADHESIVE
Resealable Pouch
• Truly Transparent   • Bonds Instantly
• Easy to Use   • Acid-Free
Glue DOTS
vellum
The Dot That Does a Lot™

⑩

expanding your stash

Once you've assembled the essentials and completed a few layouts, you'll likely want to purchase additional products. Whatever technique or effect you'd like to achieve, there's a tool, medium or accent to help. Here's a quick account of the basic categories.

TOOLS

Hand-held gear like hole and shape punches, eyelet setters, paper piercers, crimpers, bone folders, brayers and rub-on tools will simplify the scrapbooking process—and make your pages look even better.

MACHINES

Electric and manual gadgets can generate die-cut letters and shapes from dies, cartridges or computer fonts and clip art. They can also add adhesive to large surfaces, bind albums, sew on your pages and more. Before a big purchase, head to your local scrapbook store to see if you can try before you buy.

COLORANTS

Add a splash of color or a subtle tint, alter an accent, or highlight lettering or backgrounds—being artistic is easy with acrylic paint, watercolors, stamping inks, metallic rub-ons, chalks and fabric dyes.

STAMPS

Stamping is a hobby unto itself, but it can also enhance your pages with color, motifs and textures. Stamp designs in mounted, unmounted, clear acrylic and foam styles are virtually limitless. Related supplies, like heat-embossing materials, masks and specialty inks, give you even more creative options.

EMBELLISHMENTS

If you think your page needs a "little something," a quick trip to your local scrapbook or craft store will give you plenty of options. Whatever the subject, color or mood of your layout, there's a sticker, fastener, die cut, ribbon, tag, pocket, button or shape in a variety of materials to suit it.

LOVE by Lisa Bearnson. **Supplies** Patterned paper: Love, Elsie for KI Memories; Pen: Precision Pen, American Crafts; Chalk: Pebbles Inc.

TIPS FOR BEGINNERS

Before you begin, take note of the number-one rule in scrapbooking: There are no rules. The photos you use, the tales you tell, the materials you use and how you use them are entirely up to you.

It's common to feel overwhelmed at the start. Looking at your backlog of photos, the selection of supplies and even inspirational layouts in magazines may frustrate or discourage you. Don't worry. Take a deep breath and study these seven simple tips—they'll help you get organized, get motivated and, above all, get started.

① DECIDE WHAT TYPE OF ALBUM YOU'LL CREATE
Do you want your layouts compiled in a chronological family album? Separated by family member or theme? Deciding beforehand will speed the process of sorting and organizing your photos. *(For more information on albums, see Chapter 5.)*

② SORT YOUR PHOTOS
This will probably be the most time-consuming (but also the most worthwhile) task. Sift images into piles according to the album in which they'll appear, then sort further by date, event or subject. Label and store the groups until you're ready to use them. *(For more information on photo organization and storage, see Chapter 2.)*

③ DON'T SCRAPBOOK EVERY PHOTO
Save yourself time—if you have several similar pictures of your family's last get-together, for example, select the ones that best represent the event. Store the rest in a photo box or album.

④ WORK BACKWARD
It seems odd, but one of the easiest ways to scrapbook is to start with the most recent photos and slowly work back through your stash. You'll be able to remember details about the events while the memories are fresh, and completing layouts will give you an inspiring sense of accomplishment.

⑤ DON'T OVER-THINK
If you find yourself spending several hours to get a single page "just right," you may want to refocus. Concentrate on telling the story: Showcase the photos and discuss their significance rather than getting caught up in the page embellishments and the perfection trap.

⑥ DON'T OVER-BUY
Shopping for supplies is half the fun, but it can become overwhelming. Although it's handy to have a large stash, new paper and accent designs are released frequently, and styles become dated quickly. Only stock up on materials you're sure to use.

⑦ SOAK UP THE INSPIRATION
If you're stumped for a theme, title or color scheme, study the textures, sights and sounds in nature, your home, at the mall or on the road. Carry a notepad with you to record tidbits for your next scrap session. If you're particularly stumped for a design idea, turn to a page sketch—a template drawn as a "model" for a scrapbook layout. You can find sketches online or in books and scrapbook magazines.

TRIM THE TREE *by Kimber McGray.*
Supplies *Cardstock:* WorldWin; *Letter stickers:* Doodlebug Design; *Stamps:* Sugarloaf Products, Inc.; Stampabilities; *Ink:* ColorBox, Clearsnap; Stampin' Up!; *Buttons:* Autumn Leaves; *Pen:* American Crafts.

CLIMB HIGHER *by Deena Wuest.* **Supplies** *Software:* Adobe Photoshop Elements 4.0, Adobe Systems; *Digital papers:* Stockholm Simple Page Set by Anna Aspnes, *www.designerdigitals.com*; *Digital arrows:* You Are Here Brushes-n-Stamps by Katie Pertiet, *www.designerdigitals.com*; *Fonts:* Avant Garde and Establo, Internet.

saving money

Yes, you can scrapbook on a budget! With some planning, you can save a few dollars without sacrificing style.

CUSTOMIZE SUPPLIES

Don't buy every color of paint on the shelf; stick to a few basics and blend your own. Purchase stickers or chipboard letters in neutral colors and alter them with paint or ink to match specific layouts. Stamp cardstock to design your own patterned paper.

STAY ORGANIZED

Keep track of what you have and where it's located. You won't buy duplicates and are more likely to use existing supplies if they're readily available.

SAVE SCRAPS

When using cardstock as a page border, save what's leftover for another project. Scraps can make excellent accents, photo mats or borders. You can maximize even the smallest swatch with your punches and die-cutting machines.

TURN TO YOUR FRIENDS

Share supplies, split the cost of non-essential tools (like a die-cut machine) and hold swaps to trade unused materials.

GO ONLINE FOR FREEBIES

Search the Internet for free fonts, clip art and other digital elements you can use on your pages.

FIND EXTRA USES FOR USED PRODUCTS

Get double-duty from sticker and chipboard sheets—once you've used the letters or shapes, turn their negative pieces into funky titles and accents.

LOOK FOR BARGAINS

Buy supplies you know you'll always need—like adhesives—in bulk when they're on sale.

saving time

If your days are overscheduled as it is, it's important to make time to scrapbook—and use timesaving shortcuts whenever possible.

DESIGN IN STAGES

Prepare pages in your "spare time." Use 10-minute chunks to select photos, coordinate cardstock and paper, find embellishments, peruse magazines for inspiration, and jot down title and journaling ideas.

MAKE YOUR OWN PAGE KITS

Place photos in a page protector, then add paper, embellishments and notes as they're gathered. Take them to crops or to your local scrapbook store when shopping for supplies. Page design will be a breeze with the elements assembled and waiting for you.

STAY ORGANIZED

Organize and label supplies to avoid lengthy searches for that tiny embellishment you *know* you bought last week.

HANDWRITE JOURNALING

You can fill a journaling block in the time it takes you to select a font, type your text and print. Or take the ultimate shortcut—hand the pen to a family member and ask him to contribute his thoughts to the page.

KEEP PROJECTS ACCESSIBLE

If your project or layout is easy to get to, you can work on it whenever inspiration strikes. If you scrapbook in a common area of your home—like on the dining room table—place your project on a tray you can stash away between scrap sessions.

GO DIGITAL

Create a digital page—you'll be able to go start to finish without getting out or cleaning up any supplies. *(For more information on digital scrapbooking, see Chapter 9.)*

photo care and organization

One of my favorite childhood traditions was "the wall"—you know, the place where you were measured each year, a pen mark noting how much you'd grown? I love how one quick glance could reveal so much change. I love that about photographs, too—that you can flip through them and see the progression from year to year. Photos are treasures . . . they deserve to be handled with care. This chapter reveals how to keep your photographs safe.

SORTING AND STORING

What's the best way to simplify the entire scrapbooking process?
Organize your photos. Doing so now will save you time in the long
run—once you're done, you'll be able to find and access the proper
images in an instant. By following a few simple steps, you'll be
organized in no time.

❶ DESIGNATE A WORKSPACE
Locate a large area to spread photos out—and leave them
out. You'll be able to spend your time working rather than
wasting half the session taking everything out and putting
it away.

❷ GATHER ALL OF YOUR PHOTOS
Search the spots where you stash things to deal with
"later." Remove pictures from boxes, frames and damaging
magnetic albums. (Work a strand of dental floss beneath
any photos that are stuck to the pages.)

❸ SORT
Slim your photo stash, cutting down the amount you'll need
to organize and label. Separate your photographs into
three piles:

Keepers. Keepers are the shots that best represent the
event or moment; they're the ones you'll use on layouts.
They may not be technically perfect, but they do evoke
memories, record a part of family history or inspire
your creativity.

Extras. These are near duplicates and marginal photos.
You might want to hang onto them for use in gift albums
or on layouts for which you need additional images.
Another idea? Let your kids use them during craft time.

Discards. Though it's tough to get rid of any photos, you
don't have a need for those terribly out-of-focus, badly
lit or "what was I thinking?" shots. Don't waste any more
time shuffling through them.

❹ SORT AGAIN
See? Now you have just a small pile to work! Decide how
you want to organize your albums, then sort this stack into
categories to match those themes.

By Date. If you're creating chronological family albums,
sort by year. Break those piles into months or events like
holidays, milestones and vacations.

By Subject. For theme albums, classify photos by holidays, vacations, school and so forth. Further separate by
date or family member.

By Family Member. Setting up albums for individual
family members? Sift the keepers into sets for each
person. If a photo features more than one family
member, judge by the event or the "star" of the shot.
Duplicate prints come in handy here; if you don't have
them, create a "reprint" pile to order duplicates.

By Layout. If you're still not sure how you'll ultimately
arrange your pages, divide the photos into the groups
that you'll use on individual layouts. (It's not as hard as
it sounds!)

labeling

After sorting, label any photos that haven't been identified. This is important because it may be a while before you scrapbook them, and it's easy to forget the details. If the images are separated or mixed up, the descriptions will help you re-sort quickly. To ensure the labels are truly helpful, try to:

RECORD SPECIFIC DETAILS

Include as much information as possible, such as names, dates and an account of the event. If you really want to help yourself down the road, give photo sets a number, then write all of your memories about them in a notebook stored nearby.

USE A PHOTO-SAFE, PERMANENT MARKER

Never use a ballpoint pen, which can dent the snapshot. Also, don't write on the back of irreplaceable or heirloom photos—place them behind acid-free paper that includes the information instead.

ARCHIVE YOUR PHOTO NOTES ON YOUR COMPUTER

If you have a lot of images, type the data on your computer and print it out on acid-free labels with temporary adhesive.

HANDLE PHOTOS WITH CARE

If you're using a marker, let the ink dry completely before stacking the photos. If you're adding information with self-adhesive notes or labels, ensure they're completely flat and adhered only to the backs of the photos.

storage

The hard work is done . . . now for the easy part: choosing a storage system to hold your photo sets. You may want a few solutions—short-term for shots you'll be using immediately, mid-term for other "to-be-scrapbooked" images, and long-term for those you're keeping but don't plan to use. Here are several options:

BILL ORGANIZER

Numerous slots will keep photos for upcoming projects handy. The option is very short-term, however, since it will collect dust.

PAGE PROTECTORS

These are ideal if you've separated your photos by layout. Create page kits by placing photos and supplies inside, then store them in a three-ring binder.

FILE FOLDERS

Labeled folders keep sets together, yet separate. Store them in a filing cabinet, tote or lidded box.

ACCORDION FILES

Use expanding files to stow sorted photos and corresponding memorabilia. Purchase one for each year, theme or family member.

PHOTO BOXES

Stackable, lignin-free photo boxes generally hold up to 1,000 4" x 6" photos, and most feature divider tabs to maintain your filing system.

PHOTO ALBUMS

House photos in photo-safe albums with slip-in pockets. Set them on a bookshelf so images can be enjoyed even before they're on layouts.

CASES

Custom cases can hold hundreds of loose photos and several enlargements. Some feature removable boxes—a safe way to transport photos to your scrap table or crops.

PHOTO/MEMORABILIA ORGANIZERS

Specially designed organizers are ideal for safe storage of photos and negatives as well as photo CDs.

ARCHIVAL SAFETY

At the basic level, all items are made up of chemical bonds. If the bonds start to break down, the piece will begin to decompose. Knowing which elements and environments speed a photo's deterioration will help you avoid them.

ACID

Acid weakens the bonds in materials like paper and fabric, causing them to turn brown and brittle. It can also migrate to other materials. Even if you use acid-free paper, one highly acidic item on the page—may contaminate the layout and others in the album. Use a deacidification spray to treat newspaper clippings and other documents that may not be acid free.

HEAT

High temperatures can speed chemical reactions within, causing them to decay quickly.

LIGHT

Bright light—especially sunlight and fluorescent light—can hasten the deterioration process. Photos are particularly susceptible since light fades ink and bleaches colors, and because film is an inherently light-sensitive material.

CARELESS HANDLING

The transfer of dirt and oil from our hands is damaging to photos, while mishandling and improper storage can lead to scratches, wrinkles and rips. Wash your hands frequently when working with pictures, and wear cotton gloves when handling one-of-a-kind images.

We were so excited to be on our 1st cruise. The ship amazed us!

on board

January 2007. Vision of the Seas.

ON BOARD *by Leah LaMontagne.* **Supplies** *Cardstock:* Bazzill Basics Paper; *Patterned paper:* Li'l Davis Designs; *Letter stickers:* KI Memories; *Brads:* Queen & Co.; *Pen:* Zig Writer, EK Success.

preservation tips

Now that we know what can damage photos as the years pass, how can we protect them? Take care of your photos now, so your family can enjoy them for many years to come.

USE PIGMENT-BASED INKS

When printing digital photos, be sure the inks are pigment-based. Dye-based inks dry quickly but can fade or shift over time. To find the safest pairing of ink and photo paper, follow your printer manufacturer's recommendations for the longest-lasting combination.

STORE IN SAFE ENVIRONMENTS

Store your albums and photo containers away from bright light, inconsistent temperatures and high humidity.

CHOOSE ACID-FREE, PH-NEUTRAL MATERIALS

Use acid-free or pH-neutral materials and adhesives on your layouts. If you're unsure about something, analyze it with a pH-testing pen. (A pH value of 7.0 is neutral. Lower values are acidic, and higher values are alkaline—or acid free.)

AVOID PVC

Safe page protectors are manufactured with polyethylene, polypropylene or polyester.

CHECK PRODUCT SPECS

The J. Paul Getty Museum recommends verifying that anything that comes in contact with your photos (like albums, paper and storage options) has passed the American National Standard Institute's Photographic Activity Test (PAT).

DEACIDIFY AND USE BUFFERED PAPER

Slow the deterioration process of lightly acidic elements with buffered paper—it's pH-neutral and features added calcium carbonate to increase its alkalinity, which helps neutralize acid and prevents it from migrating. Materials can also be treated with a deacidification spray, which can slow the future development of acids.

FEEDING THE DUCKS by Amber Ries. **Supplies** Software: Adobe Photoshop CS2, Adobe Systems; Digital curled paper: Anna Aspnes, www.designerdigitals.com; Digital duck accent: Katie Pertiet (altered to match papers), www.designerdigitals.com; Digital frames: Instamatic Frames No. 2 by Katie Pertiet, www.designerdigitals.com; Digital drop shadows: Drop Shadow Action Set by Katie Pertiet, www.designerdigitals.com; Digital papers, doodles and photo corners: Silly Boy Cuddle Bug, www.theshabbyshoppe.com; Digital lined patterned paper: Autumn Chic, www.theshabbyshoppe.com; Digital title and journaling block: The Wonderful Collection, www.theshabbyshoppe.com; Digital rickrack: The Olivia Collection, www.theshabbyshoppe.com; Font: Pea Bailey, Internet.

protecting older photos

Although you have control over the pictures you take today, you've probably received snapshots from your childhood or heritage photos that are already in a state of disrepair. Keep the guidelines below in mind when working with them.

OLDER PHOTOS

To preserve an older photo, have a copy made at a reputable photo lab. You'll receive a new print and a negative for future reprints. Images can be scanned if you'd prefer a digital backup. Avoid photocopying older prints since the machine's intense heat may accelerate deterioration.

DAMAGED PHOTOS

If your photo is physically damaged, don't repair it yourself—you may do more harm than good. The Department of Conservation at the J. Paul Getty Museum recommends leaving repair and cleaning to a conservation specialist. To find one near you, visit the American Institute for Conservation of Historic and Artistic Works at *www.aic-faic.org*.

negatives and backups

Preserving film negatives and compact discs with digital photo backups is just as important as safeguarding the photos themselves. Without them, you won't be able to reprint favorites or replace damaged or lost prints.

BACK UP DIGITAL FILES

Back up digital files every month or after significant events. You never know when a computer malfunction might wipe out your hard drive. Industry experts recommend using high-grade recordable media like compact discs or DVDs. Avoid rewritable discs (like CD-RWs), which are less stable.

REQUEST INDEX PRINTS

Order index prints from photo developers or create your own using photo-editing software to catalog digital files. You'll be able to locate a negative or file without handling the strips or compact discs.

USE ARCHIVAL-QUALITY SLEEVES

Store negatives and compact discs in archival-quality sleeves, and make sure they're labeled—using a photo-safe marker—with the date and event. House both film and digital backups along with index prints in a three-ring binder, or check photography websites for storage boxes designed to keep out dust and light.

STORE IN SAFE ENVIRONMENTS

Store the containers in the same safe manner that you do the photos—away from bright light; inconsistent, extreme temperatures; and high humidity. And keep them away from your printed photos, either in a fireproof safe, safe-deposit box or at a relative's home. That way, if something should happen to one or the other, at least one stash will be safe.

memorabilia

Have you ever looked through a drawer—searching for a pen or scrap of paper—and come across a brochure that instantly takes you back to last summer's vacation? Souvenirs like programs and notes are the ultimate memory triggers that can help bring your photos and journaling to life. From heirlooms to modern-day mementos, here's how to find, organize and showcase these keepsakes.

WHAT TO COLLECT

While some people are naturally inclined to save souvenirs, others don't see the need. If you fall into the second group, think of collecting ephemera as finding the perfect accents for your pages—incredibly meaningful accents. Here are some ideas:

BABY KEEPSAKES

Scrapbook ultrasound photos, hospital masks, bracelets, caps and booties. Save the newspaper from the day your baby was born or a penny with the year of his birth. Keep items to illustrate milestones, like a swatch from a security blanket or a lock from his first haircut.

CHILDHOOD PAPERWORK

Save or photograph your child's favorite artwork, certificates and awards, and notes received from friends. Keep tests, handwriting samples, stories, identification cards and progress reports.

CELEBRATION MEMENTOS

Holidays, parties and special occasions have tidbits like invitations, announcements, certificates, newspaper clippings, place cards and favors. Boutonnières, corsages and flower petals can be included if preserved correctly. And don't overlook ticket stubs, receipts, cards or playbills from an anniversary or night on the town.

VACATION COLLECTIBLES

When traveling, pick up maps and brochures. Purchase postcards of sights your camera couldn't capture. Save business cards and receipts from shops and restaurants, along with hotel stationery, admission tickets or collectible buttons and pins. If you're abroad, save coins, currency and postage stamps.

EVERYDAY ARTIFACTS

The ordinary is important, too. Save a swatch of fabric from the new curtains you made or paint chips from your kitchen remodel. Gather leaves on your daily walk or shells from a trip to the beach. Keep receipts from special purchases—it'll be amusing to see how "inexpensive" they were.

The best part of staying at the Hyatt in Kauai is hanging out at the lagoon all day. One day we rented a kayak and paddled around it. The kids had such a great time! 08.07

KAYAKING FUN *by Suzy Plantamura.* **Supplies** *Cardstock:* Bazzill Basics Paper; *Patterned paper, letters and epoxy stickers:* Love, Elsie for KI Memories; *Pens:* EK Success.

what to save, what to toss

Unless you have unlimited storage space, there is such a thing as too much memorabilia. How do you keep yourself from crossing into "packrat" territory? Simple. Decide what's really worth keeping and discard the rest.

SINGLE OUT UNIQUE ITEMS

Don't save everything from a trip or event. Select what's unique to the occasion or holds special meaning to you. Do you have a story to share about it? Does it make you remember something that another souvenir doesn't?

ILLUSTRATE THE STORY

Keep items that help illustrate the story or that provide insight into what can't be seen in the pictures. Don't disregard a keepsake just because you don't have photos to go with it. Use it as the focal point on a journaling-only page.

SCAN OR PHOTOGRAPH ORIGINALS

After photographing larger pieces to use in your album, such as a child's school project, decide if you need to keep the original or if the photo is enough. Do keep what your child is especially proud of or items that showcase budding talents.

KEEP ITEMS WITH SENTIMENTAL VALUE

If a family member objects to you discarding something, hang onto it. The next time you sift through the collection, ask again—his opinion may have changed.

PRESERVE FAMILY HEIRLOOMS

Never discard a family heirloom that's been passed down to you—it may represent a family tradition or legacy that's worth passing onto your children.

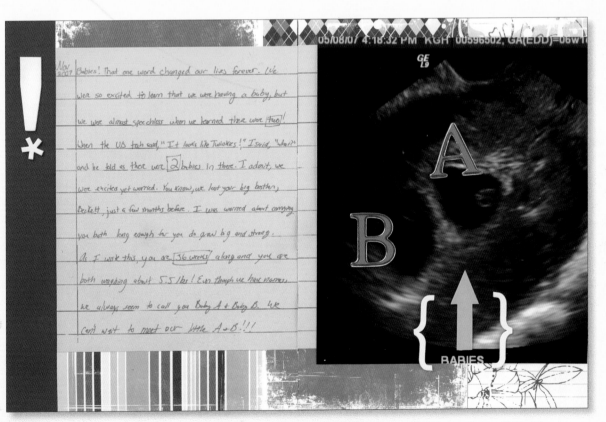

BABIES by Carey Johnson. **Supplies** Software: Adobe Photoshop CS2, Adobe Systems; Patterned paper: We R Memory Keepers; Chipboard accents: American Traditional Designs (letter) and Heidi Swapp for Advantus (punctuation and arrow); Digital brush: Old Stamps by Rhonna Farrer, www.twopeasinabucket.com.

ORGANIZING AND STORING

Now that you've chosen what to keep, where do you keep it? Organizing mementos will help preserve items and their details, and provide easy access when it's time to include them on your layouts. Try these ideas:

ADD TO PHOTO ORGANIZERS

See if your photo-organization system can accommodate the accompanying memorabilia. For example, postcards, brochures, receipts and notes can sit inside page protectors, while accordion-file pockets and photo boxes can sit alongside corresponding photos. *(See the Archival Safety section in this chapter for tips on storing acidic items such as newspaper clippings.)*

TRACK LARGER KEEPSAKES

For keepsakes stored away from photos (due to their size or to preserve the archival safety of your images), list their location and description on a scrap of cardstock and keep it with the associated pictures.

STORE LARGE ITEMS WITH CARE

Keep bulky ephemera in a sturdy, acid-free container with a lid to keep dust out. If you have a lot of memorabilia, purchase containers for each album, theme or family member.

NUMERIC SYSTEM

Try a number system: Place a number on each item, then use the numbers to reference a list of descriptions either attached to the storage box or written in a notebook housed with your photos. Record the date and data, such as the name of the person who created or owned it, where it was collected and why you think it's important.

ARCHIVAL SAFETY

Just like photos, paper documents and mementos must be handled and stored with care to prevent deterioration. Some strategies for preserving ephemera?

AVOID HEAT AND HIGH HUMIDITY

These environmental factors accelerate the deterioration of the paper fibers and cause documents to become brown and brittle. Store them in a cool, dry location where the humidity level is constant, and out of bright light, which can cause ink to fade.

USE ACID-FREE FOLDERS AND PAGE PROTECTORS

Place critical records and documents in acid-free folders or page protectors, or encapsulate them in special polyester (Mylar) envelopes. Never laminate original documents—the process is irreversible.

STORE PAGES FLAT

Folds weaken paper fibers, leading to deterioration and tearing. Never repair existing rips with tape, which is typically acidic. If the tear is particularly bad, consult a professional conservationist about repair.

DEACIDIFY

When storing multiple-page documents, treat sheets with deacidification spray, or place a piece of buffered paper between them to prevent acid migration.

REMOVE RUBBER BANDS, CLIPS AND STAPLES

These items can deteriorate or cause papers to tear with friction. If a document has staples that are rusting, slide a thin strip of stiff plastic under the fastener to prevent tearing, then use tweezers to "open" the staple and remove it.

USE A SAFE-DEPOSIT BOX

Consider housing important documents in a safe-deposit box. The environmental conditions are ideal, and they're often protected from flood and fire.

SCRAPBOOKING WITH MEMORABILIA

Although it seems impossible to include some keepsakes on your layouts, there are ways to showcase everything from a thin flower petal to a two-foot-tall trophy. But first, take steps to ensure mementos, like those listed here, are safe so they will enrich, not endanger, your albums.

IMPORTANT DOCUMENTS

The easiest treatment for certificates and other paper mementos is to photocopy the original onto acid-free paper. Although it briefly exposes the item to bright light, the benefit is worthwhile. You can share the memory and keep the original in a safe place.

ARTWORK AND SMALL PAPER MEMORABILIA

Want all the detail of your child's 11" x 18" painting? A color copy or photo will capture it . . . and you can resize the project to fit onto your layout. Preserving receipts, movie tickets or postcards? If you prefer using originals, treat with deacidification spray and affix with photo corners in case you want to remove them later. Otherwise, scanning these items gives you the flexibility to showcase them on your layout without worrying about their archival quality.

LARGE OR BULKY ITEMS

Handmade heirlooms, blessing gowns, trinkets, trophies and other priceless possessions can't be scrapbooked as is, but they can still be showcased. Photographing is the easiest way to capture detail and dimension. If possible, include shots with the person it belongs to.

FLOWERS

Dry corsages, buds or petals from meaningful bouquets with a flower dryer or flower press, or by simply placing them between blotting paper in a large, heavy book for one to two weeks. To be safe, seal them in laminate or place them in an archival-quality memorabilia pocket or vellum envelope.

NEWSPAPER CLIPPINGS

Snippets from newspapers are great scrapbook additions. However, newspaper is the first type of paper to discolor and turn brittle due to its high acid content. It's also vital to keep the acid from migrating to other documents and photos, which will hasten their deterioration. Treat the clip with deacidification spray and mount it on buffered paper with a water-based, acid-free adhesive. Or give the article its own page in your album—mount it on cardstock and stow in a page protector like a full-sized layout.

JOSHUA'S TRAIN ART *by Wendy Anderson.* **Supplies** *Cardstock:* KI Memories; *Patterned paper:* Urban Lily; *Sticker and chipboard letters:* Doodlebug Design; *Ink:* Stampin' Up!; *Ribbon:* Crate Paper and Doodlebug Design (paper ribbon); *Photo corners:* Lineco; *Font:* Smiley Monster, Internet.

what to do with it

Once your mementos are treated for photo safety, you may be in need of a little design inspiration. Check out the following ways to display memorabilia or incorporate it on your scrapbook page:

ACCENTS
Use smaller memorabilia as a page accent. Tack thick items down with adhesive dots. Or attach small items along a border, dangling from the corner of a photo frame, or alongside titles or journaling.

BACKGROUNDS
Turn a map or brochure into a page background. If you have several copies, cut one into blocks and mix with cardstock for a geometric look, into strips as a border, or into sections as individual accents.

POCKETS
Slip a collection of items like ticket stubs, receipts, cards and notes into a pocket you've created with cardstock. Just cut the cardstock to size and attach with thin strips of double-sided tape along the sides and bottom.

MINI ALBUMS
A lot of flat ephemera can be housed in a mini album made with a few tags, coin envelopes, library pockets or folded cardstock. Affix it to the corner of your page to double as a large embellishment.

SHADOW BOXES
Display larger and bulkier mementos in a shadow box—a shallow, framed box that is used for holding and protecting items on display.

CUSTOM PAGE WINDOW
Feature small items on your page by creating a custom window. Simply cut matboard or chipboard into a dimensional frame, then add a transparency as the "window." Clear memorabilia pockets have the same effect and are also self-adhesive.

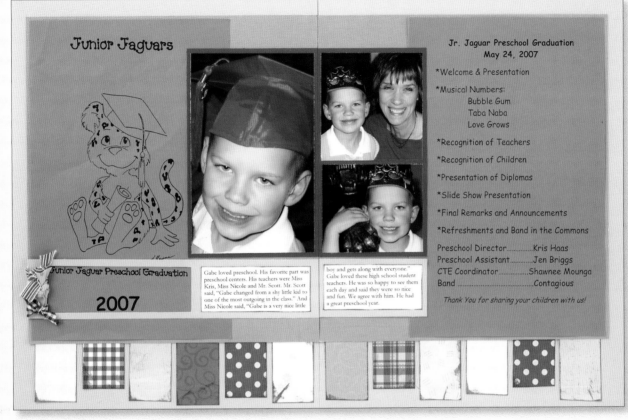

JUNIOR JAGUAR GRADUATION *by Bonnie Lotz.* **Supplies** *Patterned paper:* Chatterbox (blue swirl), Daisy D's Paper Co. (yellow), Lasting Impressions for Paper (blue dot), Provo Craft (yellow with brown dash) and Scrapbook Wizard (red papers and yellow floral); *Ribbon:* Close To My Heart (blue gingham), May Arts (red stripe) and Mrs. Grossman's (yellow dot); *Font:* Garamond, Microsoft.

DID YOU NOTICE?

You can use programs and other memorabilia from school events on your scrapbook pages. Before adding an item to your layout, either treat it with a deacidification spray or scan it and use a copy on your page instead. That way you can trim it without worrying about ruining the original.

principles of design

What constitutes an attractive page? It depends. Some love harmonious colors; others prefer clever embellishments. One might be drawn to straight lines while another opts for curves and angles. When it comes to layouts, beauty is definitely in the eye of the beholder. But most scrapbookers will agree—the best pages bring out the best in the photographs through a careful selection of colors, design elements and balance.

DESIGN BASICS

Even if you don't think you have an artistic bone in your body, you can create a scrapbook page. Whether it's your first layout or your fifty-first, you'll use the same process to produce it. Practice these steps and your signature style is sure to follow.

CHOOSE A THEME

Layouts are built around a main idea, which can be anything from a trip to Paris to a celebration of potty training. The photos, journaling, title and accents should all support the theme.

PICK PHOTOS

Sift through your "keepers" that relate to your page subject. Use close-ups, group shots and images that recount the event from start to finish.

SELECT A BACKGROUND

Cardstock and patterned-paper colors help develop the mood of the page. Place photos over different shades until you find the ones that complement your images without overpowering them.

ARRANGE THE PAGE

Determine how you want the photos to appear and select one as the focal point. Decide how much space you'll need for journaling. Aim for unity—every element should contribute to the flow, leading your eye from one image to the next.

EMBELLISH

What accents will enhance your pictures, further the theme and express your sense of style? Which techniques will add interest? Experiment, but don't go overboard. Remember, your goal is to enhance the photos, not detract from them.

UTAH HISTORY PLAY by Wendy Sue Anderson. **Supplies** Patterned paper, chipboard letters, felt flowers, paper flowers and buttons: Making Memories; Font: ScoutLightDB, www.fontplus.net.

All year, the 4th graders learned about Utah History. They learned about indians, pioneers, explorers, and mountain men. At the end of the year, they put on a play to share everything they learned. They dressed up and performed several songs and dances for us. Grandma Sweat made Meagan's cute pioneer skirt.

May 17, 2007

All i WANTED

when on bedrest was a "normal" pregnancy. Baby clothes shopping, people commenting on my belly, a baby shower, but I knew that with my high risk pregnancy, there was no way that would happen.

When I made it past 24 weeks... Amie, asked if the family could put on a shower. I knew it would have to be at my house, but I was just so happy that I would get to do this one "normal" thing!

So, at just shy of 27 weeks, I had a baby shower! Pictured: Bev, Beth, Barb, Kathy, Me, Amie, Holly and Mom. Not pictured: Kyra, Shelia and Rachelle.

SHOWER

ALL I WANTED by Carey Johnson. **Supplies** Patterned paper: K&Company; Foam letters: American Crafts; Chipboard arrow: Heidi Swapp for Advantus; Font: Arial, Microsoft; Other: Chipboard brackets.

8½" x 11" vs 12" x 12"

You have many options when it comes to creating a scrapbook layout. The most basic decision you'll make is the size of your layout. You can use 12" x 12" cardstock or the standard letter-size (8½" x 11") cardstock.

Which choice is right? In the end, it simply comes down to personal preference. You can choose to include both 8½" x 11" and 12" x 12" layouts in your albums or create separate albums depending on your page sizes. Here's a closer look at the two options:

12" x 12" PAGES

The advantage of using 12" x 12" cardstock is flexibility. The larger canvas allows more space for photos, journaling and embellishments. Additionally, most patterned papers, border stickers, transparency overlays and other scrapbooking embellishments are created for 12" x 12" pages, which makes adding them to your pages a snap.

8½" x 11" PAGES

Scrapbooking 8½" x 11" pages has its advantages as well. It's a standard letter-size so it's perfect for printing journaling directly on your pages with your home printer. In addition, 12" x 12" patterned papers and border stickers are easily trimmed to size. And while scrapbook albums are available in a variety of sizes, you also have the option of simply using a standard-size binder to store your scrapbook layouts in page protectors.

one or two pages

When creating a single-page layout, everything is contained on one page. On a "spread," you'll arrange pictures, your title, journaling and accents across two pages; when your album is open flat, the design will be visible on the left- and right-hand sides. Several factors will determine whether to go with one page or two:

PHOTOS

The page and image sizes (and how much you want to enlarge, reduce or crop) will determine the number of pictures you can fit on a layout. How many are essential to tell the story? If it's more than 3– 4, a spread will allow you to accommodate them *and* journaling and accents. If it's more than 10–12, try a series of single pages about individual aspects of the theme—for example, one page about the birthday cake, another about the gifts and so on.

JOURNALING

Plan ahead so you'll have enough space for text. Go with a spread if there are a lot of details, anecdotes and quotes to accompany your photos. Go with a single page if a small number of photos and short captions will be sufficient.

THEME

If you want to further the theme with several custom-made accents, a long title or memorabilia, you'll probably need a spread to include them.

STYLE

Do you like the flow of spreads? Dislike the look of two distinct layouts (with different color schemes and themes) facing each other in your album? Prefer the feel and speed of singles? Ultimately, you should do what makes you happy.

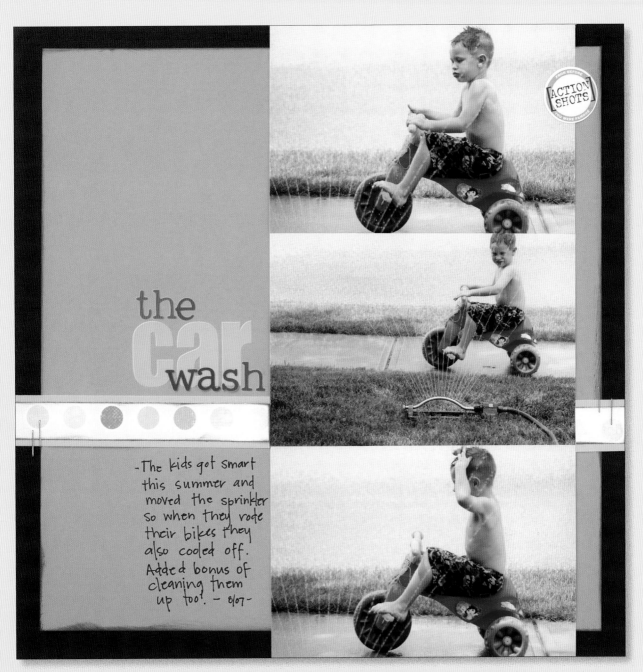

the
car
wash

- The kids got smart
this summer and
moved the sprinkler
so when they rode
their bikes they
also cooled off.
Added bonus of
cleaning them
up too! — 8/07 —

THE CAR WASH *by Kimber McGray.* **Supplies** *Cardstock:* WorldWin; *Patterned paper:* We R Memory Keepers; *Letter stickers:* Doodlebug Design and Reminisce; *Stickers:* 7gypsies; *Ink:* ColorBox, Clearsnap; *Pen:* American Crafts.

tips for spreads

The most effective two-page layouts have a unified look, the design flowing effortlessly from one page to the next as one unit. When you create a two-page layout, you want an instant, visual cue that the facing pages belong together. By using the simple techniques listed here, you can create great scrapbook spreads for your album.

FIND INSPIRATION

The best way to get started is to look through scrapbooking magazines and idea books and flag your favorite two-page layouts. Then, use those layouts as design inspiration for your layout. Notice the placement of the photos, title and journaling, and use that as the basic framework for your layout.

ADD A BORDER

Create a border around the entire spread or across the top or bottom of both pages. Try a strip of patterned paper, machine- or rub-on stitching, a thin pen line or a swipe of ink. Or let a strip of photos meet in the middle.

EXPAND THE TITLE

Place title lettering so it runs across the spread. However, don't leave too much space between words—if you use three-ring binders, you may lose continuity because of the gap between the pages.

ADD AN ENLARGEMENT

A spread is a perfect canvas for showcasing larger photos. Consider featuring a 5″ x 7″ or 8″ x 10″ enlargement of your favorite photo with additional 4″ x 6″ prints, accents and journaling to balance the design.

EXPAND A PHOTO

Your photos are the main element of your scrapbook page. By allowing a photo to bridge the gap between the two pages, you're instantly unifying them. If you're not comfortable with the idea of cutting a photo, use a color copy instead of the original. Avoid cutting the photo in critical places, such as through the subject of the photo.

BALANCE PAGE ELEMENTS

Photos, journaling, accents, white space and bold colors carry visual "weight." Place corresponding components in opposing corners, or mirror them on each side of the spread. Balance photos, too—place the largest on the left-hand page and a cluster of smaller ones on the right, for example.

REPEAT ELEMENTS

If you're designing more than two pages on a single subject, indicate they're a "set" by using the same colors and accents. Or add an image—like a stamped or chipboard arrow—to the bottom-right-hand corners as if to say, "to be continued."

USE THE RULE OF THIRDS

Envision your layout as a large tic-tac-toe grid. The locations where the lines on this grid intersect are great focal points. Keep this in mind when determining where to place photos, journaling and other important page elements.

GRANDMA'S EGG PLAN *by Wendy Anderson.* **Supplies** *Patterned paper, stickers and ribbon:* Making Memories; *Letters sticker and clip:* Doodlebug Design; *Chipboard letters:* O'Scrap!; *Font:* 2Peas Graham Cracker, *www.twopeasinabucket.com.*

DID YOU NOTICE?

Wendy balanced the two vertical photos on the left-hand page with two horizontal photos on the right.

FOCUS ON THE PHOTOS

When someone looks through your album, she probably won't scrutinize every sticker or background color. Instead, she'll most likely comment on the pictures and the memories they evoke—the true purpose of every page. Keep your snapshots in the spotlight with these design strategies that will enhance their impact:

START WITH THE BEST

Help photos attract interest by improving the photos themselves. Let the subject shine by paying attention to the background, lighting and focus as you compose each shot. *(See Chapter 7 for photography tips.)*

CROP . . . SOMETIMES

Cropping can improve photos by directing the focus to the subject. But before you trim, study what you're removing—is it a car, home or something else that might have historic value in the future? Never cut heritage photos, Polaroid prints (which may release damaging chemicals) or originals for which you have no backups.

ADD A FRAME

For emphasis, mount a photo on cardstock that contrasts with the background. Fashion an attention-grabbing frame with embossed, painted, inked, texturized or torn edges, or line one side with stamped images, doodles or text.

POSITION CAREFULLY

Use photos and elements to generate visual flow. For instance, if you have one large photo, position it off-center somewhere in the top third of the page, balancing it with smaller images, text or accents in the lower section. If possible, place photos so subjects face the center of the page—when the subject faces outward, the eye tends to follow it right off the page.

USE ACCENTS WISELY

Don't allow a large accent to steal the focus of the page. Arrange accents to direct the viewer across the layout, cluster them to help balance photos and journaling, or place them so they overlap the focal-point photo to catch the eye.

UP, UP AND AWAY *by Suzy Plantamura.* **Supplies** *Cardstock:* Bazzill Basics Paper; *Letter stickers, stickers, charms and ribbon:* Love, Elsie for KI Memories; *Pens:* EK Success and Sakura; *Other:* Patterned paper and rickrack.

USING COLOR IMAGES

There are numerous opportunities to choose colors for every page, from the background to pens to accents. Although you'll typically coordinate with the main colors in your photos, don't forget to consider these additional possibilities:

MINOR PHOTO ELEMENTS
Choose a less-dominant element in the photo and pick up its color in photo mats or other accents.

PHOTO BACKGROUNDS
Match the page color to the background of your photo if it's a solid color (like a snowy mountain or a brick wall), then adhere the image without a mat to help the subject "pop."

BACKGROUND ELEMENTS
Brighten a dark photo by using a muted, contrasting color as a page background or photo mat.

CLOTHING
Use colors that match your child or family member's clothing to help him stand out in a group shot.

COLOR WHEEL
Consult a color wheel to select combinations. Complementary colors (those situated directly opposite one another) provide the greatest contrast and can be used to draw attention. Colors adjacent to one another blend to create harmony and continuity. A monochromatic color scheme (different values of the same color) lends a subtle touch that keeps photos at the forefront.

FISHING by Leah LaMontagne. **Supplies** Cardstock: Bazzill Basics Paper and Die Cuts with a View; Patterned paper: Provo Craft; Chipboard letters and brads: Queen & Co.; Pen: Zig Writer, EK Success; Font: Times New Roman, Microsoft.

USING BLACK-AND-WHITES

You've probably got a few black-and-white photos in your ready-to-scrapbook pile, whether they're from the last century or last month. Maintain the drama and detail of the striking images with these page ideas:

GO BOLD

Don't be afraid to choose bright and complementary color combinations for your cardstock and patterned papers. Dictate the mood of the page with paper and accent colors. This will brighten up your page and add life to those older black-and-white or sepia photos.

PAIR WITH COLOR PRINTS

Add a color photo to your layout for extra emphasis. Perhaps you can combine a black-and-white studio portrait with color photos that show off more candid shots. This is also a terrific way to compare and contrast photos from the past with current photos.

PLAY WITH PATTERNS

Since you don't have to worry about matching your page colors with the colors in the photographs, don't hesitate to try patterns you might ordinarily avoid. Just be sure the colors of your cardstock and accents coordinate with the patterns. Use coordinating mats to emphasize photos.

EXPERIMENT WITH RICH, EARTHY TONES

If adding bright colors doesn't seem to match the mood or feeling you're trying to evoke (particularly with older photos), experiment with neutral shades, such as cream, olive, deep red, plum and brown.

FRAME IT UP

Add additional visual interest to black-and-white images by adding an interesting photo frame. Many different options are available in a variety of styles and materials, including felt, metal, cardstock and fabric. Adding black or colored photo corners can also add interest to an important black-and-white print.

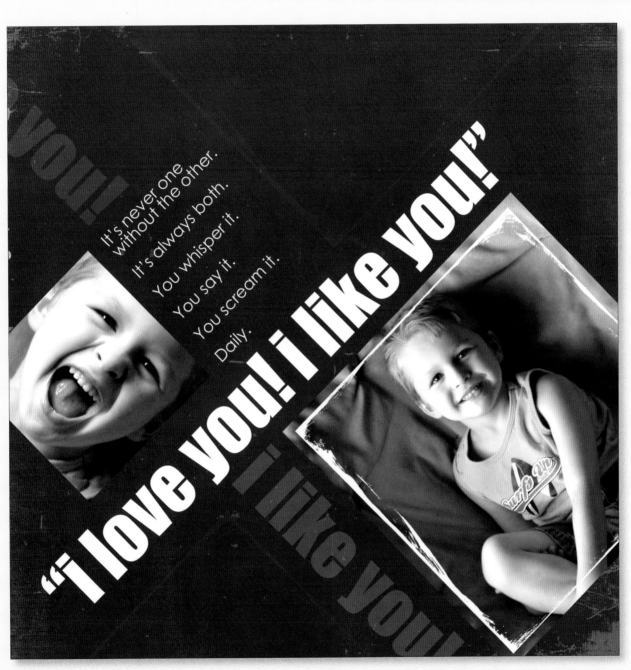

It's never one
without the other.
It's always both.
You whisper it.
You say it.
You scream it.
Daily.

"I love you! i like you!"

I LOVE YOU, I LIKE YOU *by Deena Wuest.* **Supplies** *Software:* Adobe Photoshop Elements 4.0, Adobe Systems; *Digital paper:* MonoBlendz Royale Paperie by Anna Aspnes, *www.designerdigitals.com; Digital page template:* Tortuga Template #20 by Kellie Mize, *www.designerdigitals.com; Digital frames:* Dried Brush Frames Brushes-n-Stamps by Katie Pertiet, *www.designerdigitals.com; Fonts:* Avant Garde and Impact, Internet.

developing your style

Everything from the colors of the background to the accents contribute to a layout's look. Initially, you may be unsure about what to choose. Discovering your scrapbooking taste is similar to determining your sense of fashion. Figure out your signature style by taking a look at the things you love and the styles you gravitate toward.

DESIGN INSPIRATION

Sit down with a scrapbooking magazine or idea book to choose your five favorite layouts. What do they have in common? Did you select them for their photography? Journaling style? Color combinations? Techniques? Accents?

FAVORITE FONTS

Peruse your font folder. What styles have you downloaded the most? Clean and simple sans serif? Elaborate cursive? Whimsical? Grungy? Bold?

HOME STYLE

Take note of the colors and decor in your home. Are they homey and comfortable? Trendy and cutting edge? Practical and efficient?

ADVERTISEMENTS

Think about your favorite magazine or television ads—why do they catch your attention? Humor or drama? Cleverness or basic facts?

PRODUCT INSPIRATION

Head to the sticker or rubber stamp section of the craft store. Which designs do you reach for? Are they sweet and cute? Bold and geometric? Distressed and shabby? Pretty and romantic?

PUPPY LOVE by Amber Ries. **Supplies** Software: Adobe Photoshop CS2, Adobe Systems; Digital paper (light brown): Hugs Kit by Lynn Grieveson, www.designerdigitals.com; Digital paper (dark brown): Web Freebie by Katie Pertiet, www.designerdigitals.com; Digital word-art accent: Study Hall Kit by Lynn Grieveson, www.designerdigitals.com; Digital felt letters: Feeling Blue Felt Alpha Collection by Pattie Knox, www.designerdigitals.com; Digital stitching: Stitching Holes Brushes-n-Stamps by Katie Pertiet, www.designerdigitals.com; Digital flourishes: DoodleDo Flourishes by Katie Pertiet, www.designerdigitals.com; Digital drop shadows: Drop Shadow Action Set by Katie Pertiet, www.designerdigitals.com; Digital "Love" accent: Whimsicality Series No. 2, by Jackie Eccles, www.littledreamerdesigns.com; Digital paper, buttons, ribbon and stitching: Smarshmallows, www.theshabbyshoppe.com; Digital title block: Modish Boy, www.theshabbyshoppe.com; Digital circle accents and photo-corner stamp: The Wonderful Collection, www.theshabbyshoppe.com; Font: SP You've Got Mail, Internet.

pattern three {3}

KIDS.

The
on
the form
myself "stretching
vertical photos to each lay
paper or adding additional ones.

Love
this
color
scheme
Find out which
papers she
used.

←

www.creatingkeepsakes.com   25

enjoy*

200+ ideas
for scrapbooking
your photos

EXPRESS YOUR STYLE

Scrapbooking is a creative outlet, a way to communicate your personal style. What, you don't have a "personal style"? Just relax, finish pages and have fun . . . your personality will shine through. Eventually, you may notice them fitting into a specific category, such as the ones listed below:

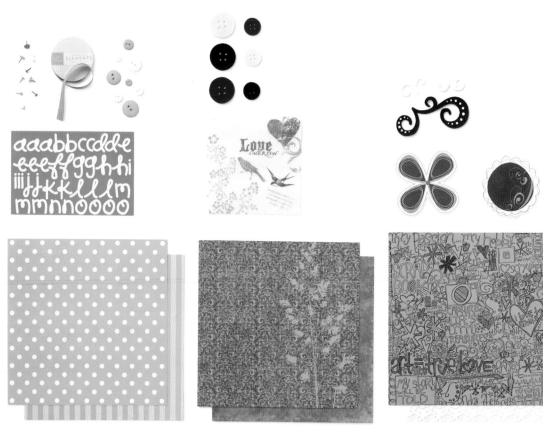

CLASSIC

Classic pages are clean and simple, featuring straight lines and an uncluttered composition. The emphasis is on the photos and journaling, with minimal embellishing.

SHABBY CHIC

Shabby chic pages have a soft, timeworn look, with distressed and crumpled edges, muted colors and adornments like stitching and hand-crafted accents.

FREESTYLE

Freestyle pages have an "eclectic" feel, with imprecise lines, hand-cut accents, doodles and whimsical embellishments.

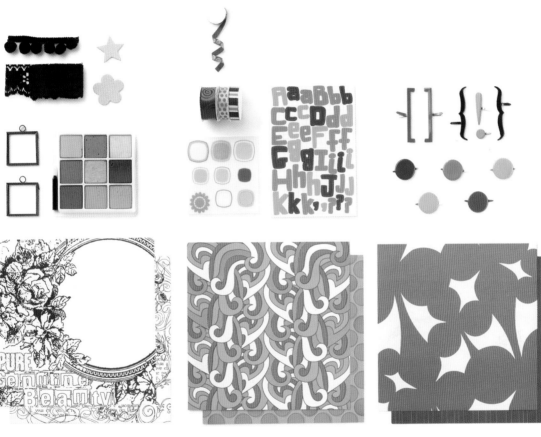

ARTISTIC
Artistic layouts are blank canvases for artistic techniques like painting, decoupage, collage and embossing.

RETRO
Retro pages turn back the clock with color combinations, angular lines and accents that are funky, yet modern.

MODERN
Modern pages feature a predominance of clean lines, geometric accents and bold, contrasting colors.

There is no deep end or slippery slide, and a diving board is simply out of the question.

Tiny POOL

It may be small but our tiny pool is the perfect size for five.

TINY POOL by Bonnie Lotz. **Supplies** *Patterned paper:* My Mind's Eye; *Chipboard letters:* Die Cuts With a View; *Rub-ons:* Doodlebug Design; *Ribbon:* Karen Foster Design (pink), Making Memories (purple rickrack), Mrs. Grossman's (yellow stripe and green dot) and SEI (red dot and pink rickrack); *Font:* Century Gothic, Microsoft.

keeping it fresh

Once you've developed that "signature style," remember: Not every layout has to fit into it. Tailoring a page's look to its photos and theme while experimenting with your tried-and-true choices will add variety and keep you creatively challenged. Don't be afraid to try different things. Here's a good start:

COLORS & PATTERNS

Go to lighter and darker shades of your usual color scheme. Using paper with different patterns (like dots when you frequently select stripes, flowers if you often reach for text) can convey a new feeling.

ACCENTS

Customize embellishments to fit the feel of your page. If you use stamps to add monograms, for example, seek out a variety of different fonts. If you love to adorn with flowers, purchase them in different materials, such as paper, chipboard and felt.

SUPPLIES

Take photos to the store and coordinate materials on the spot. Purchase paper and embellishments even if their style doesn't mesh with your usual look.

MEDIUMS

If you like to add splashes of color, change up the artistic medium you use. Dry-brush paint on one page, pounce an inkpad on another or apply chalks for a softer feel.

TECHNIQUES

Don't dismiss a new skill just because you think you won't like it. Expand your repertoire—take classes, attend workshops or participate in "make-and-takes" for opportunities to try new things.

albums

A scrapbook album will not only hold your layouts together, but protect and organize them, too. I like to compare choosing an album to buying a car (on a *much* smaller scale, of course)—you want the outside to look good, but the inside's got to be durable and functional. Learn what you need to know before you buy, and how to organize and store them once you do.

BASIC TYPES

When selecting an album, first consider the binding options. The three main types—expandable, three ring and spiral bound—are available in so many colors, textures and sizes that you won't be lacking for choices, but you'll need to decide which fits your scrapbooking and storage style best.

EXPANDABLE—POST-BOUND

Albums with expandable spines come in different styles, designed to secure page protectors within the binding of the album itself. Post-bound albums use two or three metal posts; to accommodate extra pages, simply add a few extensions.

WHAT YOU SHOULD KNOW

Post binding allows facing pages to sit seamlessly next to one another. The posts secure page protectors, so you can produce layouts on cardstock and insert them later.

Although you can add and remove pages by slipping them in and out of page protectors, to rearrange the order of the page protectors, you may have to disassemble the album.

EXPANDABLE—STRAP HINGE

Strap-hinge albums are also expand-able—two or three nylon straps slip through specially designed pages attached to staple-like loops. To add pages, remove the strap and run it through the loops in the new pages before reattaching.

WHAT YOU SHOULD KNOW

The binding allows spreads to lie completely flat with no gap between facing pages. To protect layouts, use side-loading page protectors that slip over completed pages.

Because the actual pages are bound into the book, you'll either have to create layouts directly on them or complete pages to adhere to the background later.

THREE-RING BINDERS

Operating like traditional school note-books, three-ring binders are available in small specialty sizes as well as 8½" x 11" and 12" x 12". Purchase one with D-shaped rings, which allow the pages to lie flat when the book is closed. Versions sold at craft stores feature longer covers to prevent pages from extending beyond the edges of the album.

WHAT YOU SHOULD KNOW

It's easy to add, remove and rearrange pages—simply snap the rings open and closed. Buying 12" x 12" will allow you to mix page sizes in the same album since both 12" x 12" and 8½" x 11" page protectors will fit.

SPIRAL BOUND

Spiral-bound albums attach pages permanently to a wire coil. As with three-ring and expandable styles, spiral books are offered in a range of sizes and covers. Pages are exposed, unless you purchase a variety with bound page protectors in place of cardstock or one that comes with side-loading page protectors.

WHAT YOU SHOULD KNOW

Inexpensive and limited in size, it's easy to complete an album in a day. Ideal as theme or gift albums, spiral books have the added benefit of the coil, a handy place for decorative ribbon ties or other adornments.

ALBUM ARRANGEMENT

To make layouts easier to find and enjoy, it's important to determine how they'll be organized and stored within your albums. Before you decide, think about the type of pages you plan to create, how many versions you want to work on, your storage space and what will happen to the keepsakes in the future. Consider these options:

family member

1 One common way to designate albums is by person. Family members will have books filled with their milestones, moments and favorites. Again, the layouts within each album will most likely be organized chronologically.

WHAT YOU SHOULD KNOW
Children will feel a sense of pride looking through their own albums. And, once they're grown, they won't have to worry about dividing up the family albums.

theme

2 If you tend to scrapbook subjects that fall into the same categories—such as holidays, school or home—try theme albums. Dedicate an entire book to "vacations," for example, to house layouts of your travels, day trips and excursions. You'll probably want to combine systems, further arranging layouts chronologically, as well.

WHAT YOU SHOULD KNOW
Theme albums are enjoyable to look at, allowing you to instantly see changes and growth from year to year. They may be easier to create if you decide on an overall color or embellishment scheme since you'll have fewer choices when you begin each page.

chronological

3 Many scrapbookers like to compile all-in-one family albums arranged by date. Regardless of subject or family member, every layout will sit within the same album in January–December order. This system follows the natural flow of time, which provides an invaluable historical record for future generations.

WHAT YOU SHOULD KNOW
With a chronological album, it's easy to locate a layout if you know the date of the event. Photos are in one place, so you won't have to keep track of different albums. Every layout subject will have a "home," and you may have fewer albums to store overall.

MINI ALBUMS

Any album smaller than 8½" x 11" is referred to as a "mini album." Ranging in size from 9" x 9" down to 2" x 2", those on the larger end are available in three-ring, expandable and spiral-bound styles with page protector, cardstock, chipboard or transparency pages. Smaller books typically feature staple or ribbon-bound cardstock pages. But if you're feeling creative, you can craft your own out of one of the following:

SCRAPS

Trim cardstock scraps to the height and two times the width of each page. Score and fold along the center, punch holes at both ends and tie with ribbon.

TAGS

Group a bunch of shipping, fabric or metal-rimmed tags and string them together with beaded chain, jute or colorful ribbon. Turn them into individual, tiny layouts.

PAPER BAGS

Stack a few brown paper bags, fold in half, staple along the folded edge to bind, then trim off the other ends. While not acid free, this is a great project to make with kids. Decorate and use bag "pockets" to hold memorabilia, journaling and more!

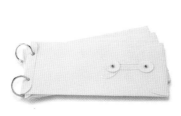

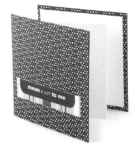

LIBRARY POCKETS

Punch holes along the left side of several library pockets and bind with ribbon or brads. Adorn the fronts and slip small photos inside.

ENVELOPES

Punch holes along the closed end of a handful of envelopes—sold in scrapbook stores in a variety of colors, sizes and closures—and connect with small binder rings.

CARDSTOCK

Create an accordion album from a single sheet of cardstock. Just trim and fold the cardstock (as you would a fan), adhering chipboard to both ends as covers.

project ideas

But what can you do with a mini album? More than you think! The process is empowering—you can focus on one subject, look at the project as a whole when choosing designs and techniques . . . and complete an entire album in one sitting, if desired. Gather your photos, supplies and just pick a theme!

ABC

Teach the alphabet with a personalized book. Designate one page per letter and fill with photos, stickers and other embellishments that start with that letter.

SCHOOL

Record each year with a "school memories" book. Mount a class picture on the left-hand page and lined paper on the right. Ask your child to write about highlights and favorites (collecting a handwriting sample in the process).

I LOVE YOU

Combine cherished photos with a list of reasons why you (or your kids) love the recipient. Include special touches like your child's handprint and handwritten notes and memorabilia.

VACATION

Chronicle your complete journey with photos, postcards, your itinerary, packing lists and journal entries.

TEACHER

As the perfect end-of-the-year or teacher-appreciation gift, take (or ask parents for) a photo of each child in the class and have them draw something or write a quick thank-you next to their picture.

RECIPE

Build heirloom recipe books with instructions, photos of finished dishes and tips. Put one together for different phases of the meal: appetizers, soups, salads, entrees, side dishes and desserts.

GIRLS JUST WANT TO HAVE FUN
by Suzy Plantamura. **Supplies** Cardstock: Bazzill Basics Paper; Patterned paper: American Traditional Designs, Autumn Leaves, KI Memories and Paper Salon; Velvet paper and circle stickers: SEI; Rub-ons: Déjà Views by The C-Thru Ruler Co. (words), Doodlebug Design (letters) and me & my BIG ideas (glittered); Glaze: Diamond Glaze, JudiKins; Glitter: Stampendous!; Felt flowers and chipboard flower buttons: Maya Road; Chipboard accents: me & my BIG ideas and SEI (frame); Library pocket: Li'l Davis Designs; Epoxy buttons and ribbon: KI Memories; Embroidery floss: DMC; Buttons: Autumn Leaves; Brads: Queen & Co.; Pens: EK Success (pink) and Sakura (white); Other: Vellum envelope and chipboard album.

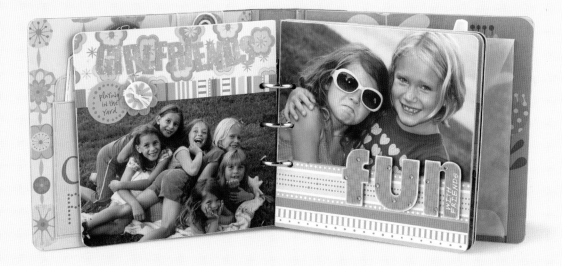

ALBUM DISPLAY

Where you'll store completed albums hinges on one question: Do you want to tuck albums away (safe for posterity) or leave them out for family and friends to enjoy today? Once you've decided, your options include:

BOOKSHELVES

Pick one with adjustable shelves so you can store a range of sizes. Label the spines—some feature a clear pocket to hold a cardstock tag, while spiral albums allow you to tie a name to the coil. Add titles to plain albums with letter stickers, rub-ons or characters stamped with solvent ink.

COOKBOOK STANDS

If you like to have your work on display, use a cookbook stand. Place one in your scrap space or on your mantel where visitors can check out your recent layouts and family memories.

BASKETS

An assortment of mini albums can be clustered in baskets of all shapes and sizes. Rotate them often to give guests new artwork to view—and to keep projects relatively dust-free.

TOTES

Several scrapbook-supply manufacturers offer tote bags specially designed to hold albums up to 12″ x 12″—a convenient way to transport them to family gatherings or to crops while they're still in progress.

CASES

Check your local craft or container shop for archival-quality album cases. Featuring lids to keep dust at bay, most are sturdy enough to stack.

COFFEE TABLE

Place your most recent layouts in an album you can set out on a coffee table so the entire family (and guests) can enjoy reliving the recent adventures you've scrapbooked!

The Easter Bunny brought Andrew a scooter. The next thing you knew was he had grabbed his helmet and ran outside despite the 30° weather. "Mom, watch me do my stunts!" Ok, so your stunts involved riding in the grass instead of on the sidewalk and kicking your scooter out in front as you jumped off. Crazy kid!

Easter '07

stuntman

STUNTMAN *by Kimber McGray.* **Supplies** *Cardstock:* WorldWin; *Patterned paper:* Carolee's Creations and Cosmo Cricket; *Letter stickers:* American Crafts; *Ink:* VersaMagic, Tsukineko; *Chipboard accents:* American Crafts and WorldWin; *Pen:* Zig Writer, EK Success.

DID YOU NOTICE?
Kimber inked around the edges of her cardstock background for a distressed effect.

archival safety

When all is said and done, a finished album isn't just a collection of your family's memories, it's a culmination of your creative effort. Protect your treasure from the elements so it can be enjoyed by future generations. Pay particular attention to:

DIRECT SUNLIGHT

Although the supplies you purchase at scrapbooking retailers are considered "fade proof," keeping albums away from direct natural light sources will ensure they're protected against harmful UV rays.

DUST

Prevent micro scratches in photos and page protectors by dusting albums regularly, stashing them away from vents or storing them in individual cases. Purchase styles that are compatible with page protectors to keep photos covered.

EXCESSIVE TEMPERATURE CHANGES

Store your albums in a location that is insulated from temperature fluctuations. Rather than storing them in a garage or an unfinished basement, where they may experience sweltering heat in the summer and freezing temperatures in the winter, place them inside your home in a room where temperatures remain relatively constant.

MOISTURE

Find a storage spot that's cool and dry to prevent warping and mildew.

WEIGHT

Don't stack loose albums on top of one another—the pressure may lead dimensional embellishments to dent facing photos and pages. Keep books upright with plenty of "breathing room" in between.

MINI ALBUMS

Store mini albums and other creative album projects separately. If you have albums you've created with your scrapbooking and art supplies just for fun (and not for archival safety), consider storing them separately from the albums you are storing for archival purposes. Over time, you want to ensure that the non-archival projects do not affect the albums you intend for long-term preservation.

tools and techniques

Preserving family memories makes scrapbooking rewarding, but playing with all of the tools and supplies makes it *fun*. Who can resist the rich colors, eye-catching patterns, funky shapes and touchable textures? You're only limited by your imagination when it comes to what you can do with them. This chapter will familiarize you with the basics and give you a sampling of the creative opportunities they afford you.

CARDSTOCK AND PATTERNED PAPER

Paper is an essential supply, so it's a good thing it's available in hundreds of colors, designs and textures. (If you're unsure about a piece's acidity, double-check with a pH-testing pen to be safe.) Once you build up a large paper stash, separate it by color, theme or manufacturer and store it in vertical paper holders, horizontal trays, totes or hanging and accordion files.

paper types

Whether you use paper as your page base or as an embellishment, you have many material and color choices. Determine the best option for your project by considering how you want to use it and how you want it to coordinate with your other page elements.

CARDSTOCK
Heavy-weight, acid-free paper that serves as the base for a scrapbook layout. Available in many varieties of colors, textures, patterns and weights.

PATTERNED PAPER
Acid-free paper available in a range of colors, patterns and themes for use as page backgrounds, accents, photo mats and more.

SPECIALTY PAPER
Includes a variety of handmade, embossed, flocked and glittered papers to add a special touch to pages. Available in a variety of textures and weights.

CORK
Lightweight sheets of bark that add texture and dimension to scrapbook layouts and other craft projects.

VELLUM
A semi-translucent paper available in a variety of colors and textures. Great for layering over photos, journaling and more.

TRANSPARENCIES
Clear and preprinted acetate sheets used as overlays, windows and page backgrounds.

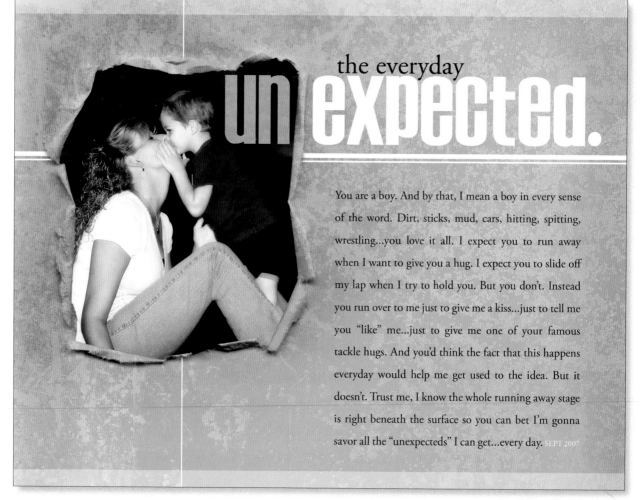

the everyday unEXPECTED.

You are a boy. And by that, I mean a boy in every sense of the word. Dirt, sticks, mud, cars, hitting, spitting, wrestling...you love it all. I expect you to run away when I want to give you a hug. I expect you to slide off my lap when I try to hold you. But you don't. Instead you run over to me just to give me a kiss...just to tell me you "like" me...just to give me one of your famous tackle hugs. And you'd think the fact that this happens everyday would help me get used to the idea. But it doesn't. Trust me, I know the whole running away stage is right beneath the surface so you can bet I'm gonna savor all the "unexpecteds" I can get...every day. SEPT 2007

THE EVERYDAY UNEXPECTED *by Deena Wuest.* **Supplies** *Software:* Adobe Photoshop Elements 4.0, Adobe Systems; *Digital paper:* Winterfest Solids by Jesse Edwards, *www.designerdigitals.com*; *Digital frames:* Torn Frame Overlays No. 1 by Anna Aspnes, *www.designerdigitals.com*; *Fonts:* Adobe Garamond Pro, Adobe Systems; Establo, Internet.

DID YOU NOTICE?

Deena cut her patterned paper so she could place her photo behind it, then she curled back the edges around her photo for a cool dimensional effect.

basic uses and tips

Paper isn't just a great base for a scrapbook layout. Consider these other practical ways to make the most of this basic supply.

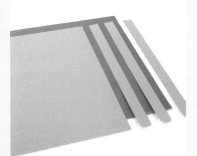

BACKGROUNDS

Solid weight and a host of colors make cardstock ideal for background pages. Use it whole or cut a few shades into blocks or strips and reassemble them for a color-blocked design. Patterned paper can also become a backdrop, but back it with cardstock for stability.

PHOTO MATS

Images get added definition when backed with coordinating or contrasting cardstock or patterned paper. Place your photo over the matting material, determine how wide you'd like the mat to be, draw tic marks with a pencil, then cut with a paper trimmer or craft knife.

ACCENTS AND CARDS

Save your paper scraps for hand-cut lettering, borders, and title and journaling blocks. Turn larger leftovers into handmade cards and gift tags. Smaller portions are great for die-cut machines and punches.

TEARING

Create a decorative edge by tearing instead of trimming. Tear paper dry for a rough edge, or paint a line of water, score or rip along a ruler for a smooth edge.

SANDING

Resurface your patterned paper and white-core cardstock by using sandpaper or steel wool to distress the surface.

CRUMPLING

Texturize cardstock, patterned paper or die cuts by crumpling them. Work slowly from the outside in to avoid tearing.

BASIC CUTTING TOOLS

You know you're a scrapbooker when . . . you discover a pile of brightly colored cardstock and paper scraps at your feet. You'll spend a good part of every scrapbook session with your cutting tools—cropping photos, trimming cardstock, creating handmade accents. Here's a closer look at what you may want in your arsenal.

❶ PUNCHES

Punch out special designs or basic shapes with these hand-held tools. Available in a variety of designs as well as squares and circles, punches cut out the designated shape with the push of a button. Hand-held hole punches are primarily used to make holes for fasteners or bindings.

❷ CORNER ROUNDER

For curved edges, use this hand-held punch to quickly and easily round 90-degree corners on photos, photo mats, papers and more.

❸ STRAIGHT SCISSORS

Regular straight-edge scissors are ideal for cutting traced shapes, snipping ribbon and more. Choose from a variety of handle styles.

❹ DECORATIVE-EDGE SCISSORS

These scissors produce decorative edges like scallops, deckled designs and zigzags.

❺ SELF-HEALING MAT

This flexible cutting surface won't wear down, even after multiple cuts. Protect your work surface by placing the mat down before cutting photos and papers with a craft knife.

❻ RULER

For straight cuts and edges, keep a stainless-steel ruler on hand to measure your cuts and line up your craft knife.

❼ SHAPE CUTTER

This swivel knife or custom blade works with templates for cutting large circles, ovals and other basic shapes.

❽ T-SQUARE

This drafting tool will help in marking and making long, straight cuts.

❾ SCORING TOOL

Use this tool with templates to create fold lines on cards and other projects.

❿ CRAFT KNIFE

This sharp utility knife is designed to make straight cuts in combination with a ruler. Use over a self-healing mat to protect your work surface.

⓫ TEMPLATES

These special templates are used with a swivel knife or custom blade to create large circles, ovals and other basic shapes.

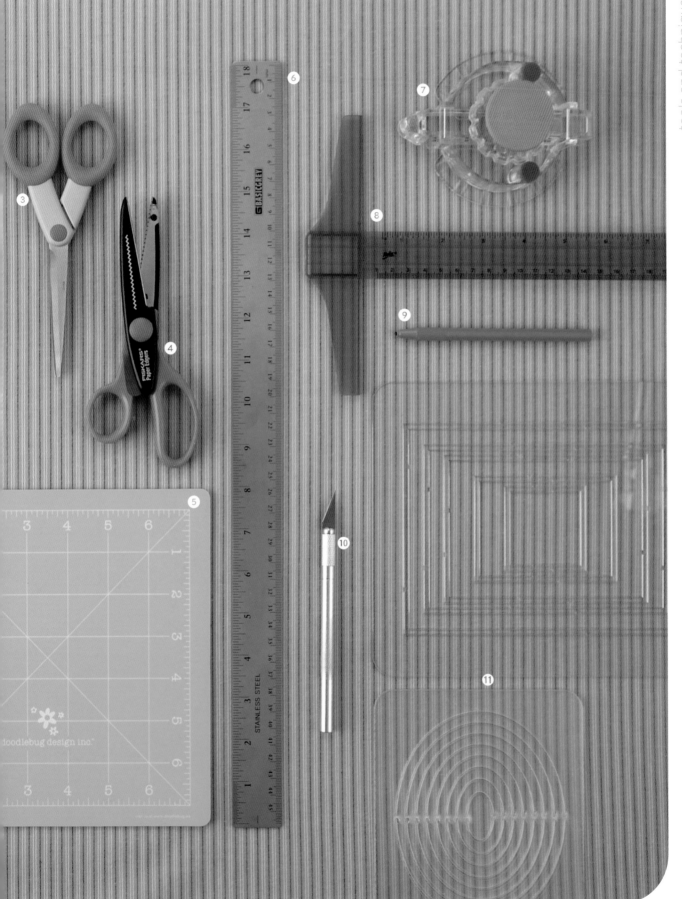

DIE-CUT MACHINES

From intricately cut designs to lettering, die-cut machines allow you to add the look of perfectly cut titles and accents while saving you time.

HANDHELD MANUAL DIE-CUT MACHINE

Create cuts or dry-emboss by pressing down on a handle, which presses a metal die through paper.

TABLETOP DIE-CUT MACHINE

Larger than the handheld unit, this device is operated by a handle or crank to push the metal dies through paper.

ELECTRIC DIE-CUT MACHINE

This electronic unit cuts shapes with the press of a button. Some models include cartridges with designs, while others use fonts or clip art straight from your computer.

TRIMMERS

Make quick work of cutting photos and papers with paper trimmers. Consider these options:

PERSONAL TRIMMER

Portable trimmer with a safety blade housed in a guide arm attached to the base at both ends. Push the blade along the cutting track to trim.

ROTARY TRIMMER

Device with a rolling blade for cutting. Offered in portable and tabletop designs, with a guide arm that secures the item while cutting. Blades are often interchangeable, with scoring and decorative styles.

GUILLOTINE TRIMMER

Trimmer with a long blade hinged at the top that swings up and down to cut.

Jared was excited to race his orange #13 car in his very first pinewood derby. The car didnt even make it past the finish line on the first heat, but after a few adjustments it was going strong. He was more than thrilled when the results were announced and he won first place!

PINEWOOD DERBY *by Bonnie Lotz.* **Supplies** *Letter stickers:* The Paper Loft; *Brads:* Making Memories; *Font:* CK Newsprint, www.scrapnfonts.com; *Other:* Circle punches.

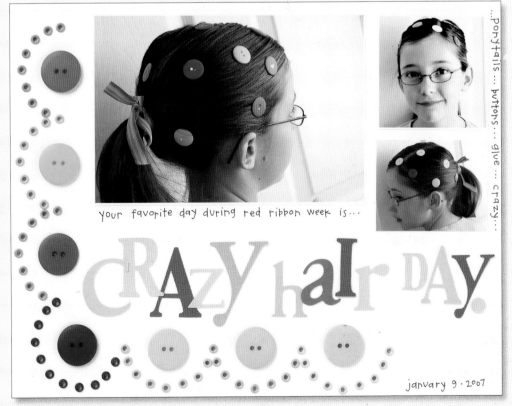

your favorite day during red ribbon week is...

...ponytails ... buttons ... glue ... crazy...

CRAZY hair DAY.

january 9 · 2007

CRAZY HAIR DAY *by Wendy Anderson.* **Supplies** *Cardstock:* Bazzill Basics Paper and Die Cuts With a View; *Buttons:* Making Memories; *Eyelets:* Doodlebug Design; *Pen:* American Crafts.

Christmas 2006 was different than most. We had just lost Beckett in Nov, & we were not sure how to mourn his loss and still celebrate the season with family. I wasn't able to take photos with the Johnson family, too many kids and it was just too hard, but I did take photos on Christmas Eve at my parents. It was a nice quiet adult Christmas - Subtle and yet warm. Just what we needed. Bob & I also spent time at Lura Lake with the dogs before it got dark.

It was different ... but good.

Christmas 2006

CHRISTMAS 2006 *by Carey Johnson.* **Supplies** *Patterned paper:* K&Company; *Clips:* Memory Makers; *Brads:* Stemma; *Font:* Arial, Microsoft.

basic uses and tips

Cutting tools are great multi-taskers. Master these basics to get the most out of your cutting supplies.

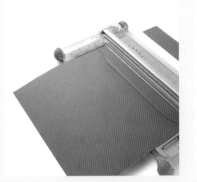

CROPS

Cardstock, patterned paper and photos can be instantly and perfectly trimmed. Die-cut machines and punches can also quickly crop pictures into simple shapes.

EDGES

Add variety to borders, page edges and photo mats with decorative-edge scissors or punches (turn them upside down to gauge exactly where you're punching).

TITLES AND ACCENTS

Die-cut machines and punches make quick work of titles and accents because there's no need to trace and cut.

TEXTURIZING

Check the capabilities of your die-cut machine—many can generate shapes from chipboard, fabric or thin metal sheets for added texture.

SCORING

Get more use from cutting tools by using them to create bases and adornments for handmade greeting cards. Change the blade in your trimmer to score cards so they're easier to fold, as well.

MAINTAINING

Change blades often to keep cuts crisp. If your cropped photos have frayed white edges, for example, your trimmer needs a new blade. Service scissors and punches by cutting wax paper or aluminum foil periodically.

PENS AND PENCILS

One of the most basic tools is also the most versatile: A single pen can be used to journal, add doodles and highlight accents. Luckily, you won't have to settle for one—or even one color, tip style or effect. Group markers and colored pencils by color or tip type, and store in baskets, cups or cases. Keep pencils tip-side up to prevent breaks, double-tipped markers horizontal to keep both sides "juicy," and all others tip-side down.

pen types

Not every type of pen is safe for your scrapbook. To prevent smearing, fading and possible damage to your photos, keep these considerations in mind when shopping:

PERMANENCE
Use permanent-ink pens that are resistant to water, light or chemicals. Look for brands labeled waterproof, lightfast and chemical resistant.

ARCHIVAL QUALITY
Inks should be photo safe, non-toxic and acid free.

INK
Dye-based ink can fade over time, so look for pens with pigment-based inks.

WRITING SURFACE
Consider the combination of your pen and paper and what may lead to bleeding or seeping. When writing on glossy paper or transparencies, for example, look for a pen with solvent ink that will dry quickly.

lettering styles

When hand-lettering (or choosing a computer, stamp, sticker or rub-on font, for that matter), the style is defined by characteristics that affect the overall feel of your page, such as:

SHAPE
Evoke different moods with a font's shape. For instance, rounded letters and long, sweeping strokes contribute to a softer, elegant feeling, while defined, simple letters convey a modern look.

SERIFS
Some lettering styles, like Times New Roman, have "serifs," small markings at the end of each letter stroke. Others, such as Century Gothic, are "sans serif" and offer a cleaner feel.

WEIGHT
Letters can be made up of fine lines or broad strokes. Bold block lettering, for instance, is imposing but less refined than thinner fonts, while outline styles are whimsical and informal.

He is like a big kid in the water.

NEVER QUIT!

wild & crazy

brad 7·06

WILD & CRAZY by Wendy Anderson. **Supplies** *Cardstock:* Die Cuts With a View; *Patterned paper:* Art Warehouse, Creative Imaginations; *Letter stickers:* Doodlebug Design and Making Memories; *Chipboard stickers:* Making Memories; *Colored pencils:* EK Success and Sanford; *Eyelets:* Doodlebug Design; *Ribbon:* O'Scrap!.

basic uses and tips

You can use your stash of pens to do so much more than simply write journaling. Try these different ideas to get the most from your supplies.

TITLES

Use pens to freehand titles, trace template lettering or outline acetate or chipboard letters. Use pencils to color or add shading to letter stickers or die cuts.

JOURNALING

Help your handwriting look its best with a flattering tip size (ranging from .001 to .8) and style (such as fine, chisel, calligraphy or bullet). Draw guidelines with pencil, or write the text in pencil and trace over it with a pen.

DOODLES

Add swoops, swirls and creative graffiti to backgrounds with markers, paint or opaque gel pens.

TEXTURIZING

Play with the way you add color to a shape. Instead of solid color, use "hatch marks" (parallel lines drawn close together) or "stippling" (a series of dots in varying sizes).

PAINTING

Use watercolor pencils to paint titles or softly shade cardstock accents. Just draw like you would with a colored pencil, then blend with a wet paintbrush.

COORDINATING

Use pens to enhance and unify premade embellishments. Coordinate titles with different styles (or colors) of letter stickers by tracing around each letter with the same ink color.

STAMPS

Stamping is a simple way to add designs, text and texture. Choose from images, frames, borders, patterns, shadow shapes, words, journaling blocks, letters and numbers in an array of sizes and styles. Sort and stash stamps on open shelving or in baskets, shallow drawers, boxes or stamp tote bags according to type, theme, size or manufacturer.

stamp types

You have many choices when it comes to adding to your stamp collection. Stamps fall into three broad categories. Depending on your personal preferences and specific needs, you'll find each has its own unique advantages.

1 POLYMER-BASED (PHOTOPOLYMER)

Often called acrylic stamps, these clear stamps are unmounted. The material is naturally clingy, which allows it to temporarily adhere to an acrylic block for stamping. Because the stamp is clear, it's easy to position images and letters on your page for perfect placement.

2 FOAM

A great, inexpensive stamping option, foam stamps work well for larger designs and for stamping with acrylic paint.

3 RUBBER

Rubber stamps are available in a vast selection of designs. You can purchase ready-to-use mounted rubber stamps or unmounted stamps. Unmounted stamps are images carved into rubber sheets that must be trimmed and mounted—temporarily or permanently—on a wood or acrylic base before use.

typical anna

14 years old April 29, '07

Making one of her famous mega water balloons! She's been making them for years!

That's Anna for ya... always playin' around! It is no wonder why the little kids love her so much; she sure knows how to have fun! She is still such a kid-at-heart. We all love being around her, she makes us want to play too! Thanks for being you, Anna.

TYPICAL ANNA by Leah LaMontagne. **Supplies** *Cardstock:* Bazzill Basics Paper and The Paper Company; *Stamps:* CherryArte and Technique Tuesday; *Ink:* Stampin' Up!; *Pen:* Zig Writer, EK Success; *Buttons:* Making Memories.

① ② ③

fall

eat
cake
© 2006 STAMPIN' UP!

basic uses and tips

Stamps are so versatile, you'll wonder how you ever got by without them. Create your own custom titles, accents and more. Here are other ideas to keep in mind.

EMBOSS

Add dimension and texture to stamped images by embossing them. Simply follow the steps on page 94.

STAMP A TITLE

When stamping titles or journaling, you'll never have to worry about running out of letters! Use letter stamps to create entire titles or mix and match with letter stickers.

STAMP AN IMAGE

Create a unique accent for your page by stamping an image with an ink that coordinates with the colors of your layout or photo.

RESURFACING

Fashion new looks for bold designs by inking the stamp and pressing a textured item (like bubble wrap) onto the surface before stamping. The texture will lift away a bit of the ink, leaving a unique pattern.

GRADATING

For titles, stamp some letters immediately after they've been inked and others after they've been pressed lightly onto scrap paper first. The variation in shades will add subtle dimension.

CLEANING

When stamping with ink, clean stamps with damp paper towels, paint pads (available at paint and hardware stores) spritzed with stamp cleaner or baby wipes. Paint will require water and a stiff brush, while solvent ink needs a special cleaning solution, available at craft stores.

HEAT EMBOSSING TOOLS

With just a few basic supplies, you can make your stamp collection even more functional by creating embossed images. Here's what you'll need.

STAMPS
Stamp designs, such as an image, letter or background, are perfect for creating an embossed effect.

EMBOSSING INKPAD
This clear or slightly tinted sticky ink is designed for use with embossing powder.

EMBOSSING INK
Embossing ink is available in bottles with sponge dauber tips for direct-to-stamp application.

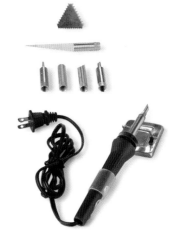

EMBOSSING POWDER
This fine powder melts to produce a raised image.

EMBOSSING GUN
This hand-held electric tool blows hot air on a concentrated spot to melt embossing powder or enamel.

EMBOSSING TOOL
Pour embossing powder on your cardstock, then write, draw or doodle with this tool to create embossed designs.

HEAT EMBOSSING

When you're ready to step it up, get extra mileage from your stamps with heat embossing. The glossy, raised designs will add texture to your pages and greeting cards. Here's how:

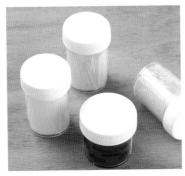

① CHOOSE EMBOSSING POWDER

Embossing powder is available in diverse colors and finishes, including sheer, opaque and metallic. After heat-setting it, it has a raised appearance like you'd see on a professional business card.

② SELECT INK

Pigment or embossing inks are ideal because they stay wet long enough for the embossing powder to stick. Choose a pigment ink in a shade that's lighter or matches the embossing powder. Embossing ink is clear, so unless you want a clear image, choose colored embossing powder.

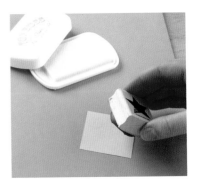

③ INK AND STAMP

Work on a large piece of scrap paper to catch excess embossing powder. To prevent powder from sticking to other parts of the background, rub the paper with an anti-static bag or a used dryer sheet. Then ink your stamp and press onto the surface.

④ ADD POWDER

Sprinkle embossing powder over the image and gently tap the paper to remove the excess.

⑤ HEAT

Use an electric embossing (or heat) gun to melt the embossing powder. (A regular blow dryer won't produce enough concentrated heat to do the job.) Hold it a few inches above the design and move it slowly until the powder has completely melted. Hold small pieces with tongs so you don't burn your fingers!

Cagney in her
Halloween costume
October 2007

Fairy
Princess
butterfly

FAIRY PRINCESS BUTTERFLY by Bonnie Lotz. **Supplies** *Patterned paper:* Daisy D's Paper Co.; *Letter stickers:* K&Company; *Stamps, rub-ons, rickrack, buttons and butterfly:* Making Memories; *Brad:* Hot Off The Press; *Butterfly clip:* Nunn Design; *Font:* CK Girl, www.scrapnfonts.com.

DID YOU NOTICE?
Bonnie added a cluster of flowers on the left side of her focal-point
photo to balance the smaller photos on the right side of it.

MEDIUMS: PAINTS, INKS AND CHALKS

Color. It's one of the first elements to catch the eye and one of the easiest—and most fun—to experiment with. Acrylic paints, watercolors, stamping ink, chalk, metallic rub-ons, alcohol inks and fabric dyes . . . it's time to get your hands dirty! Organize coloring mediums by type, shade or effect, then use them to custom-design accents or completely alter existing ones.

paint types

Paint adds an artistic element to your scrapbook layouts. Choose paint according to the desired effect and type of material.

ACRYLIC
Acrylic paints have a matte finish and come in rich opaque colors. Use on cardstock, patterned paper, chipboard, acrylic accents and more.

SPECIALTY ACYRLIC PAINT
In addition to the basic solid colors, acrylic paints also offer an array of specialty options, including glitter, metallic, glossy and pearlescent finishes.

SPRAY
For coated and non-porous substances, use these high-gloss enamel paints.

WATERCOLOR
For an artistic effect, watercolor paint is translucent and offers a matte finish. Use on watercolor paper or heavy cardstock.

paint applicators

Are you adding just a bit of paint to your page or a whole lot? Here are your options for adding a splash of paint to your pages.

MAKEUP APPLICATORS
For easy control when applying to small surfaces. Disposable and cheap.

SPONGES
For dabbing a small amount of paint at a time, creating a textured look.

PAINT BRUSHES
Best for fine application and detail work.

FOAM BRUSHES
For applying paint to larger surfaces and areas, including page backgrounds and large accents.

FOAM STAMPS
For stamping letters, flourishes and more.

ink and chalk types

Ink varieties vary in their properties, drying times and advantages. You may want several shades of each type. Check out these types of ink and chalk, as well as some tools you'll need:

1 PIGMENT POWDER

Loose powder with a metallic finish. Apply over watermark or pigment ink, or mix with a binder like gum arabic and paint with it.

2 WATERMARK INK

Gummy, clear pigment ink. Generates tone-on-tone images. Allow to dry as is, or heat emboss or brush with chalk.

3 PAINTBRUSH

Use with pigment powder to apply over stamped images.

4 TWEEZERS

Use to dip items in dye to keep hands clean.

5 DYES

Powder that is mixed with water to create a dye. Dip cardstock, silk flowers, tags, ribbon and more.

6 PIGMENT INK

Slow-drying, fade-resistant and permanent. Perfect for heat embossing.

7 DYE INK

Water-based ink that dries quickly. Available in a wide range of colors.

8 CHALK

Pigment ink that dries to a soft, powdery and often opaque finish.

9 SOLVENT INK

Permanent ink formulated to dry quickly on slick surfaces like transparencies, metal and plastic.

10 ALCOHOL INK

Use this ink on nonporous surfaces, such as acrylic, transparencies and glass embellishments.

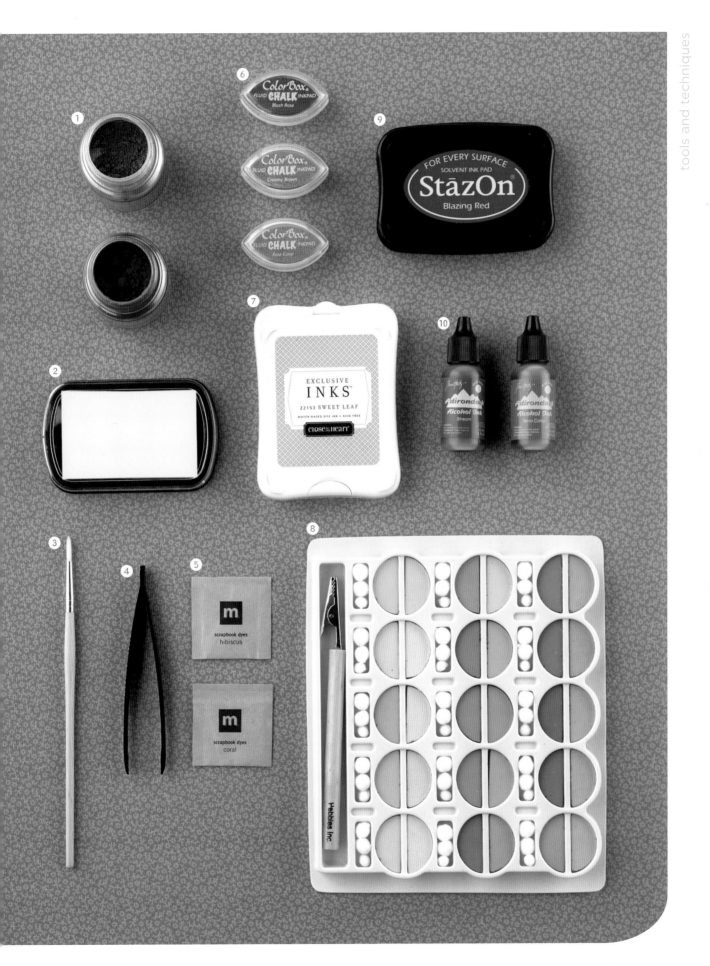

PLAYING IN THE SNOW *by Suzy Plantamura*. **Supplies** *Cardstock:* Bazzill Basics Paper; *Foam letters:* American Crafts; *Chipboard letters and snowflakes:* Maya Road; *Ink:* Clearsnap and Tsukineko; *Pens:* Sakura.

DID YOU NOTICE?

Suzy grouped her snowflake accents in two sets of three to balance
this two-page layout.

basic uses and tips

Paints, inks and chalks allow you to add an artistic touch (and color) to your page elements. Here are some other ideas for making the best use of these supplies.

STAMP

Use stamping ink with rubber and clear stamps. For foam stamps, use acrylic paint. If you want to add chalk and rub-ons to stamped images, use a watermark ink.

SHADE

Colorize backgrounds or alter stickers, rub-ons and die cuts by swirling with chalk. Build color slowly rather than applying one heavy layer.

HIGHLIGHT

Give backgrounds, photo mats and die cuts a punch of color by dry-brushing acrylic paint, swiping ink or rubbing chalk along the edges.

WASHING

Dilute paints or dyes with water and use as a wash of color for patterned paper, stickers and die cuts.

TEXTURIZING

Apply paint in new ways. Spatter with a toothbrush, dab on with bubble wrap or a sea sponge, or apply over mesh (remove the mesh before the paint dries).

ADDING BLING

Sprinkle glitter pigment powder or microbeads over wet paint, dimensional adhesive or glaze before it dries.

TEMPLATES

Without extremely steady hands, drawing a perfect circle (or an oval or a star or an outline letter "g") can be a challenge. But there's a trick to crafting a great shape with minimal effort: a template. Organize plastic, chipboard and brass templates by type and theme. Store them in binders or in hanging files for easy access (place paper between each template to prevent snagging).

template types

PLASTIC
Inexpensive and available in a wide variety of styles, including letters, shapes and dimensional shapes, such as envelopes and boxes.

CHIPBOARD
Dual-purpose chipboard pieces can work as templates or as an actual page embellishment.

BRASS
Durable and the perfect thickness for dry embossing. Available in many intricate designs.

template tools

❶ PEN
Use to trace template designs on a background.

❷ CRAFT BLADE
Use with templates to make precise cuts in cardstock.

❸ FOAM BRUSH
Use to apply paint on cardstock using the template as a mask.

❹ EMBOSSING STYLUS
Use with templates to create raised surfaces.

he Press, Inc.
97013 • 800-227-9595
HINA

For more ideas, visit our website
www.paperpizazz.com

MAKE A WISH *by Kimber McGray.* **Supplies** *Cardstock:* WorldWin; *Patterned paper:* Scenic Route; *Stamp:* Autumn Leaves; *Ink:* Ranger Industries; VersaColor, Tsukineko; *Glitter glue:* Stickles, Ranger Industries; *Chipboard accents:* Fancy Pants Designs and Maya Road; *Pen:* American Crafts.

DID YOU NOTICE?

Kimber used the negative pieces of a chipboard flower as a stencil by placing them over the background and filling in the open designs with glitter glue.

basic uses and tips

Templates are a great reusable resource. Experiment by using your templates for something new with these ideas.

ACCENTS

Trace the shape from a template onto the back of your chosen material (to hide pencil lines) and trim with sharp scissors or a craft knife.

STENCILS

Although they're often used to help cut, stencils can be traced directly onto the background as a motif. Take it further by holding the stencil in place, then pouncing with paint, chalk or ink to "fill in" the design.

DRY EMBOSSING

Set a brass (or even plastic) template on a light box, place a sheet of cardstock over the design and use a metal stylus to trace the image. Adhere it with the shape popped out or with the recessed side up (also known as "debossing").

PAPER PIECING

Cut a template shape in several colors of cardstock or patterned paper, snip them apart, then reassemble as a layered, paper-pieced design.

REVERSING

Turn your template into a mask: Cut out a shape, affix it to the background with temporary adhesive, then press ink or apply paint around the image. Remove the mask to let the background show through.

RESIZING

If your template shape isn't large enough, trace the shape onto scrap paper, then photocopy and enlarge it onto the back of your desired paper.

STICKERS AND DIE CUTS

Whatever your style—cute, eclectic, funky, elegant or classic—there's a sticker or die cut to suit it. Use letters, shapes, motifs and text to add a subtle touch or build an entire page theme. These accents are available in a variety of sizes, shades and materials, including cardstock, fabric, felt, epoxy, foam and chipboard. Divide by color, design, theme or manufacturer and store in drawers, files or binders.

sticker types

Stickers are available in a wide-range of materials and textures, giving you the ultimate flexibility to choose styles to match your layout.

❶ CARDSTOCK
Thicker paper, typically with a matte finish.

❷ EPOXY
Plastic coating with a bubble-like dimensional appearance.

❸ TRADITIONAL
Usually glossy appearance.

❹ FOAM, FELT, VINYL
Dimensional, adhesive-backed die-cut shapes, letters or images.

❺ SPECIALTY
Mixed-media, layered elements combining felt, rubber, cardstock and other materials and backed with adhesive.

die-cut types

Die cuts are available in a variety of materials and textures. Choose styles to match your layout.

❻ CHIPBOARD
Available "raw" (gray) or coated (white, solid color or printed).

❼ GLITTERED CHIPBOARD
Chipboard with a colored glittered coating.

❽ PRINTED CARDSTOCK
Printed punch-out designs, such as tags and journaling, on cardstock.

❾ PRINTED, PRECUT CARDSTOCK
Precut cardstock die cuts; no perforations or punch-outs necessary.

❿ PRINTED CHIPBOARD
Printed, punch-out designs on chipboard.

⓫ DIE-CUT CARDSTOCK
Cardstock die cuts created using a die-cut machine (see page 82 for more information on die-cut machines).

⓬ SPECIALTY PRINTED CARDSTOCK
Printed cardstock with flocking, foil or glittered images.

1

2

3

4

5

6

7 shimmer jigsaw.
pre-glittered chipboard flowers

green & purple
44 flowers

8

heidi
grace
designs

9 **baby**

10

master tags

ally's wonderland

11

12 locked
tags
diecut punchouts

E IS FOR ESCAPE *by Kimber McGray.* **Supplies** *Cardstock:* WorldWin; *Patterned paper:* Scenic Route; *Stickers:* 7gypsies; *Photo corners:* Heidi Swapp for Advantus; *Brads:* Making Memories; *Pens:* Zig Writer, EK Success; Stampin' Up!.

DID YOU NOTICE?

Die-cut tabs are a simple way to dress up photos on a layout. Kimber added tabs
to the photos on the top half of her layout and wrote captions next to them.

basic uses and tips

Stickers and die cuts make embellishing your scrapbook pages quick and easy.
Here are some basic ways to use these scrapbooking staples.

ACCENTS

Cluster them in small groups or
overlap other page elements for a
well-balanced effect.

TITLES

Use letter stickers in various materials,
mix and match colors and cases, or
blend in a few shape stickers (a sun
for the letter "o," for example) to
add interest.

FRAMES AND CAPTIONS

Align a row of stickers, word stickers
or long die cuts to design a unique
photo frame or page border. For a
quick caption, place a word or quote
sticker above or below the photo.

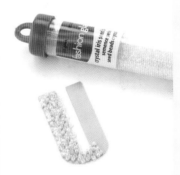

DISTRESSING

Age and add texture to stickers by
crumpling, roughing up with fine-grain
sandpaper, using paint or ink to recol-
or specific portions, or washing with
watercolors or dye.

ELEVATING

Neutralize the sticker's original adhesive by brushing it with cornstarch,
then affix it with dimensional foam
tape for a raised effect.

BEADING

Add sparkle: Coat the top of a sticker
or die cut with double-sided adhesive
or a thin layer of glaze before pressing
it into clear microbeads.

RUB-ONS

With the look of digital graphics and the versatility of stickers, rub-ons can go where stickers won't adhere and a computer printer can't reach. Apply everything from stylish text to faux stitching onto paper, fabric, transparencies and even dimensional accents like buttons and brads. Whether they're stored in files, drawers or binders, rub-on sheets can be grouped by color, style or manufacturer.

rub-on types

❶ LETTERS
Available on sheets; sometimes perforated for ease of use. Great for titles and journaling.

❷ NUMBERS & ICONS
Available on sheets; sometimes perforated for ease of use. Great for layering over photos and for card-making.

❸ IMAGES
Decorative images and flourishes. Great for embellishing photos, titles and more.

❹ WORDS AND FULL-COLOR DESIGNS
Decorative words and phrases. Great for accents and titles.

HALLOWEEN COSTUMES by Suzy Plantamura. **Supplies** *Patterned paper:* Junkitz; *Rub-ons:* Daisy D's Paper Co. (title and date circle), Die Cuts With a View (stitching) and Hambly Studios (journaling block); *Felt stars and chipboard arrow:* Maya Road; *Digital frames:* Toy Camera Frames by Tia Bennett, *www.twopeasinabucket.com*; Pens: Sakura.

basic uses and tips

Rub-ons are so versatile—you can easily add them to other premade accents for a completely new effect. Here are some other ideas to try.

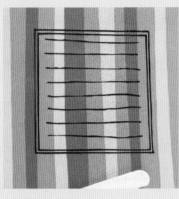

ACCENTS

Use a Popsicle stick or embossing stylus to apply rub-ons to backgrounds and other page elements. Keep surrounding areas covered to stop strays. Use a photo tab or tape to rub and gently lift away any "mistakes."

JOURNALING

Create your own quick and easy journaling spot with rub-on journaling lines.

EMBELLISH PHOTOS

If you're not a digital scrapbooker, use rub-ons to achieve the look of designs layered onto photos. Apply with a blunt tool and only on duplicate images.

ALTERING

Punch tiny shapes into bold rub-ons with a handheld hole punch, crack designs before adhering or recolor images with chalk.

DISTRESSING

Adhere rub-ons to textured cardstock, then sand carefully to reveal the background for a worn or painted look.

SAVING MONEY

If you run out of frequently used letters, snip others apart to reproduce them—for example, an "n" easily becomes an "r." Staple the backing sheet to your rub-ons immediately so designs won't stick to other supplies in your stash.

RIBBON AND FLOSS

What was once a trimming for packages has become a versatile embellishment. Ribbon and other "string-like" items, such as jute, embroidery floss, raffia and twill, are multi-functional accents that introduce color, dimension and texture. Separate ribbon and fibers by color, design or width and store spools in drawers, on rods or on vertical paper towel holders. Loose lengths look great in jars, on floss cards or looped onto binder rings.

ribbon and floss types

❶ TWILL
Textured ribbon with a textile weave that looks like diagonal lines. Great for altering with dyes or stamps.

❷ SPECIALTY
Includes stitched or printed ribbon, usually grosgrain or satin.

❸ GROSGRAIN
Close-woven ribbon available in a variety of widths. Widely available.

❹ RICKRACK
Flat-braid trim woven to form zigzags. Available in a variety of styles and widths. Great as borders.

❺ FIBER
Available in a wide variety of textures and styles.

❻ EMBROIDERY FLOSS
Loosely twisted thread available in a wide color range. Great for hand-stitching elements onto scrapbook pages.

❼ JUTE
Coarse, strong fiber with a natural look. Use to tie or string small charms and accents on a page.

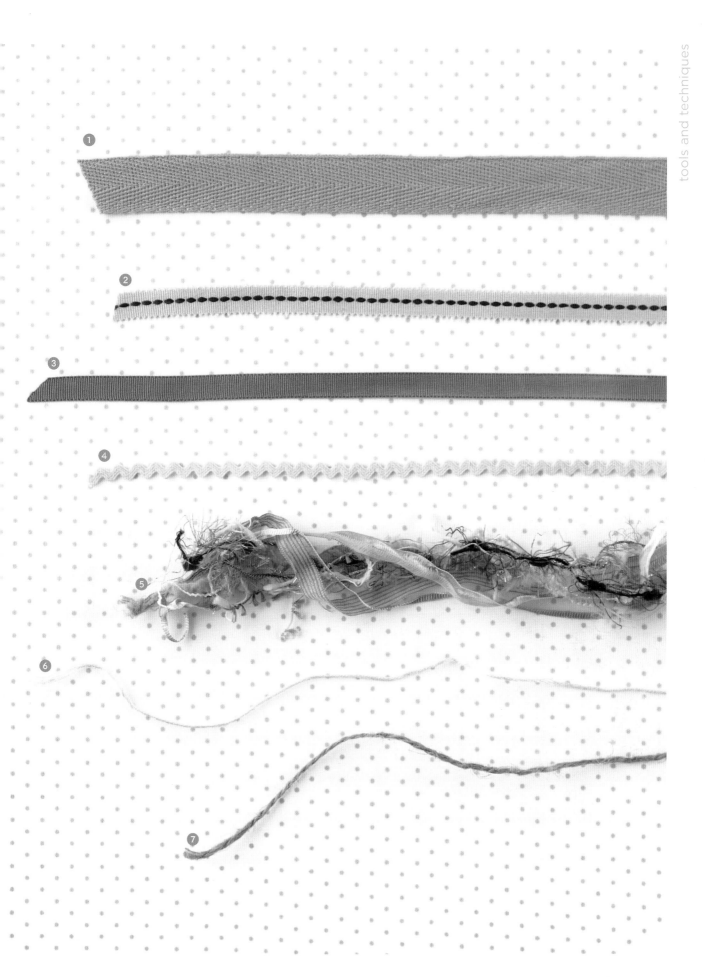

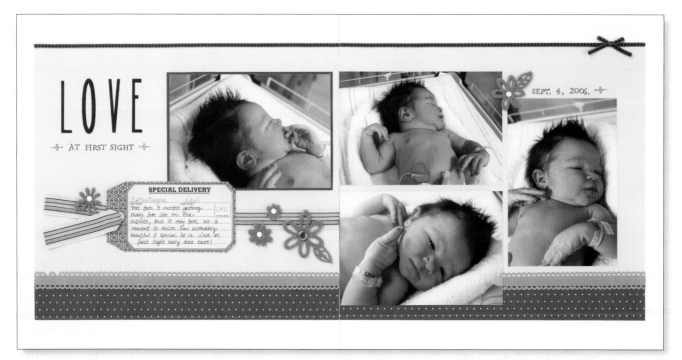

LOVE AT FIRST SIGHT *by Leah LaMontagne.* **Supplies** *Cardstock:* Bazzill Basics Paper and Die Cuts With a View; *Patterned paper:* Chatterbox and KI Memories; *Letter stickers:* Chatterbox; *Stamps:* Hero Arts and Technique Tuesday; *Ink:* Stampin' Up!; *Ribbon:* SEI, Making Memories and Michaels; *Felt flowers and white brads:* Queen & Co.; *Jewel brads:* Jo-Ann Scrap Essentials; *Tag:* 7gypsies; *Pens:* Zig Writer, EK Success.

DID YOU NOTICE?

Ribbon also makes a great border. Leah used ribbon to create a border along the top of her page, adding a bow in the top-right corner.

basic uses and tips

Adding ribbon and floss to a scrapbook page is a great way to add a handmade touch to your design. Here are some other ideas to try.

TIES

Use ribbon functionally to "hang" or group tags, tie segments of a color-blocked background together or bind a mini album.

KNOTS

Add a decorative touch with short lengths of knotted ribbon tied to page elements, as photo corners, as flower centers or along the spine of a spiral-bound album.

STITCHES

Lend a homespun look to die cuts, journaling blocks and borders by sewing along the edges with embroidery floss or thin ribbon.

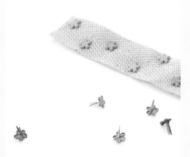

CUSTOMIZING

Add stitching, paint, fasteners and even text (with rub-ons or stamps).

WEAVING

Design backgrounds with a loosely woven "mat" of ribbon, or use a punch to create a pattern through which you can thread ribbon or fabric strips.

FRAYING

Give ribbon a funky treatment by pulling threads to loosen and fray. If you'd rather keep ends clean, however, brush with glaze to seal them.

EMBELLISHMENTS

You'll be like a kid in a candy store when shopping for embellishments—cool little doodads in an array of shades, shapes and textures that can add personality to your pages. The main types include fasteners (brads, eyelets, clips and snaps), flowers, buttons, beads, charms, labels, tags and bookplates. Organize embellishments by type, design, color, theme or manufacturer within tins, tilt bins, baskets or bead boxes.

embellishement types

❶ FASTENERS
Decorative and functional accents, including buttons, brads, clips and eyelets.

❷ FLOWERS
Available in a variety of materials and textures, including silk, paper, felt and more. Attach with adhesive or brads.

❸ CHARMS
Shaped metal accents that attach to layouts with brads, jump rings or adhesive.

❹ TAGS, LABELS AND JOURNALING CARDS
Great for adding captions and journaling to pages.

❺ GEMS, SEQUINS AND GLITTER
Add sparkle and glitz to pages with rhinestones, sequins, glitter and more.

have fun!

blow
out
the
candles

make
a wish

happy birthday!

sugar coating
swimming pool glitter

sugar coating
bubblegum glitter

NOVEMBER 2007

I SUPPOSE I COULD WRITE IT AGAIN AND AGAIN HOW MUCH SHE LOVES HER LITTLE BROTHER - AND I WILL TOO, BECAUSE IT SURPRISED ME, AND STILL DOES SURPRISE ME, THAT SHE HAS SO MUCH LOVE AND SO MUCH PATIENCE - CONSIDERING THE FACT THAT HE CAME ALONG AND TURNED HER WORLD ON ITS HEAD. BUT LOVE HIM SHE DOES, ALMOST TOO MUCH. THANKS TO HER, HIS LITTLE PARTS ARE NEVER SAFE FROM POKING, AND HE CAN NEVER DEPEND ON A GOOD AFTERNOON NAP IF SHE IS NEARBY. WHEN HE CRIES SHE DOESN'T MAKE FACES, RUN AWAY OR CRY HERSELF. NO, SHE VERY CARINGLY RUBS HIS BELLY AND SHHHHS HIM. YES HE CAME ALONG AND LIFE CHANGED DRAMATICALLY, BUT THANK GOODNESS, SHE LOVES HIM ANYWAY.

SHE LOVES HIM ANYWAY

SHE LOVES HIM ANYWAY *by Amber Ries.* **Supplies** *Software:* Adobe Photoshop CS2, Adobe Systems; *Digital paper:* Little Creepers Kit (stripe and black) by Mindy Terasawa, *www.designerdigitals.com; Digital buttons:* Autumn Glory Kit (beige) by Mindy Terasawa, *www.designerdigitals.com;* Primarily Buttons (green and purple) by Katie Pertiet, *www.designerdigitals.com; Digital frame:* Krafty Frames by Katie Pertiet, *www.designerdigitals.com; Digital torn paper edges:* Simple Torn Edges No. 2 by Anna Aspnes, *www.designerdigitals.com; Digital ribbon:* All Bunched Up Ribbon Pack and Sheridan Kit (green) by Katie Pertiet, *www.designerdigitals.com; Digital drop shadows:* Drop Shadow Action Set by Katie Pertiet, *www.designerdigitals.com; Digital letters:* Battered Alphabet by Lynn Grieveson, *www.designerdigitals.com; Digital staples:* Summer Breeze Kit by Lynn Grieveson, *www.designerdigitals.com; Digital arrows:* Megaset Arrows (black arrow) by Tracy Robinson, *www.tracyanndigitalart.com;* Altered Arrows No. 1 (purple arrow) by Jackie Eckles, *www.littledreamerdesigns.com; Digital paper:* Smell My Feet (notebook paper), *www.theshabbyshoppe.com; Digital stitching:* Harvest Spice, *www.shabbyprincess.com; Font:* Pea Lacy, Internet.

basic uses and tips

Embellishments are just that—supplies to embellish your pages. And the possibilities are literally endless. Here are some other ideas for putting these great products to good use.

ACCENTS

Use embellishments for what they were intended—as ornamental touches, of course! Find designs that coordinate with the mood of your page.

FASTENERS

Decoratively affix journaling blocks, ribbon, bookplates and more with brads, eyelets, nailheads and snaps.

CORNERS

Cluster a group of flowers, tags or buttons overlapping the corner of a photo, title block or background page.

ALTERING

Recolor paper with paint or ink. Sand plastic for a distressed look. Resurface metal by heating with an embossing gun and dipping it in embossing powder.

LAYERING

Use accents to adorn your accents! Experiment with combinations like brads as flower centers, clear buttons as windows for stickers and more.

STAMPING

Yes, you can stamp on them, but you can also stamp *with* them. Pounce an inkpad on flowers, buttons or chipboard shapes, then press the item onto your page to leave a cool impression.

photography

A good photo is like a good book—it sets a scene, evokes a mood and, above all, tells a story. I'm always amazed at the emotion a great photographer can reveal through a single image. And while you obviously don't have to be a professional to capture moments for your scrapbook, making the most of your camera's features and brushing up on photography basics is a straightforward way to improve your results.

DIGITAL SLR

DIGITAL POINT-AND-SHOOT

FILM SLR

CAMERAS

Do you remember your first camera? You'd turn the flash on, press the shutter . . . then hope you'd get a few keepers from each roll of 24. Today, whether you choose a digital or film point-and-shoot or single-lens reflex (SLR) camera, you'll get a more intuitive system, better picture quality and a host of options to give you greater creative control.

point-and-shoot

Digital and film point-and-shoot cameras are fully automatic, compact and lightweight. These days, even basic models include features that you can select or customize, such as:

AUTO FOCUS
Take quick snapshots without worrying about adjusting the focus.

ZOOM
Get closer to your subject without moving an inch.

SHOOTING MODES
Pick the setting to suit the type of image you're taking.

FLASH
Use different modes, like red-eye reduction or fill flash to assist in different conditions.

SELF TIMER
Set up and snap a photo, but be in the shot at the same time.

IMAGE QUALITY
Choose the size of your digital photo files.

VIDEO
Shoot video directly with your digital camera.

single-lens reflex (slr)

In general, SLR cameras give you higher-quality images than point-and-shoot models. And they give you extra control in addition to all the features of a point-and-shoot (minus the video):

MANUAL FOCUS
Focus the shot rather than leaving it up to the camera and lens.

ISO
ISO refers to the film speed, which determines its sensitivity to light. Some point-and-shoots let you select the ISO, but SLRs offer a greater range.

APERTURE
This setting controls the amount of light let into the camera, which affects the depth of field and exposure.

SHUTTER SPEED
The shutter speed determines the amount of time light is let into the camera, which affects the focus of moving objects.

LENSES
Change lenses for convenience, distance or effects. Examples include wide-angle, zoom, telephoto and macro lenses.

FLASH
Add an auxiliary flash for greater lighting control.

OPTIONS
Customize multiple settings that affect your photos, such as tone, hue, sharpness, color space, white balance and many more.

purchase considerations

With all the models on the market, which should you get? I asked photography expert Candice Stringham to list features she considers when buying an SLR or point-and-shoot.

MEGAPIXELS

Whether it's an SLR or point-and-shoot, check megapixels first—they determine how big you can print an image and still have it look good. Find the one in your price range with the highest amount of megapixels.

SLR

Pick a system you can build on. Is it a camera that can grow with you? Does the company have additional lenses you'll want to buy? Look at the body's construction—will it hold up over time?

POINT-AND-SHOOT

Because the lens isn't interchangeable, be sure it has a good optical zoom and covers the distance you need. (Disregard "digital zoom," which just blows up the image, reducing quality.) Press the shutter to determine lag time—the shorter the better.

advantages of digital

With the flexibility digital cameras afford, film models have taken a backseat, whether the photographer is an amateur or a seasoned professional. According to Candice, digital helps improve your photography in several ways:

IMMEDIATE RESULTS

You get instant results and can retake the shot if you need to.

EASE OF USE

It's easy to practice new techniques. There's no extra film or wasted developing costs when you take a lot of pictures.

ISO FLEXIBILITY

You can change the ISO between shots to suit the conditions. With film, you'd have to finish an entire roll before switching to one with a different ISO.

ADJUSTABLE WHITE BALANCE

You can change the white balance on every shot if needed.

EASY PHOTO FIXES

You can use Photoshop or other photo-editing programs to enhance your images.

SHORT COURSE ON PHOTOGRAPHY

It bears repeating: One of the best ways to make your pages look better is to improve the photos on them. Don't worry about advanced techniques if you're just starting out. But do learn the fundamentals and practice, practice, practice.

the manual

In order to implement the basics, you should be familiar with your camera's features and settings. Study the manual to find out about:

SHOOTING MODES

What modes—such as portrait, night or action—are available? What symbols signify them? For example, on some SLR cameras, "A" means "automatic," while on others it stands for "aperture priority."

 AUTOMATIC: Ideal for most point-and-shoot photos—shutter speed and aperture are set automatically for a wide range of shots.

 SCENE/LANDSCAPE: Ideal for taking full-frame images at a distance while keeping the entire scene in focus.

 PORTRAIT: Ideal for taking portraits by keeping the foreground subject in focus.

 ACTION: Ideal for taking sports or action shots—a faster shutter speed freezes the action.

 MACRO: Ideal for close-ups of small subjects like flowers or insects.

 NIGHT: Ideal for photographing in darker settings—the longer shutter speed helps capture light, so hold the camera steady or use a tripod to eliminate camera shake.

SNOW/BEACH: Ideal for taking photos in bright light reflected off snow or sand.

controls

How can you change the ISO? Turn the flash on and off? Master the simple functions so you can complete them in a pinch. Here are some to pay attention to:

FOCUS DISTANCE

What's the minimum and maximum distance you can stand from your subject and have the shot be in focus?

FLASH RANGE

How far can you stand from your subject and still light it properly? A standard camera flash will reach about 15 feet.

cole, you absolutely shine in the sunshine!
with your white blonde curls and bright
swim wear you looked just like a little
surfer dude. The summer when you were
two (2007) was full of many opportunities
to look cute in the water! we spent
time at the South Jordan Aquatic
center, cherry Hill, a week
at Lake Tahoe and many
afternoons in our little
pool at home!
surfs up!

AWESOME LITTLE DUDE *by Bonnie Lotz.* **Supplies** *Patterned paper:* Bo-Bunny Press; *Rub-ons:* Sonburn; *Brad and tag:* Making Memories; *Ribbon:* May Arts; *Font:* CK Handprint, *www.scrapnfonts.com.*

focus

No one likes a blurry picture (unless it's taken that way for artistic effect). Consider a few factors that contribute to a photo's focus:

APERTURE

Aperture determines the amount of light that's let into the camera and what portion of your image is in focus. A smaller aperture—with an f-stop of 32, for example—may result in an overall sharp image, while a larger aperture of 1.8 will have your subject in focus with a blurred foreground and background. The larger the number, the more your photo will be in focus.

SHUTTER SPEED

Controlling the amount of time light is let into the camera, shutter speed affects the focus of a moving subject. A fast speed, such as 1/1000 will freeze movement, while a slower speed of 1/60 will result in a blurred subject.

CAMERA SHAKE

Keep the camera as steady as possible—plant your feet, tuck your elbows in and roll your finger over the shutter button, rather than stabbing at it. This is especially important if you use a point-and-shoot and have no control over the other factors.

exposure

Are your photos too dark? Completely washed out? It's all determined by exposure—the combination of aperture and shutter speed. If you're using an SLR, consult your camera's manual to see how to adjust them. But if you're shooting in "automatic" mode or with a point-and-shoot, other factors can influence the exposure:

LIGHTING

The quality of light plays a crucial role in how well an image turns out—your subject should be well lit, but avoid intense lighting, which will lead to squinting and harsh shadows. Overcast and even rainy days are ideal for outdoor photos, generating softer lighting that flatters skin tones and makes colors vibrant. *(Read more about lighting conditions in the Q&A at the end of this chapter.)*

FLASH

Flash lighting helps freeze action to produce sharper images but can wash features out and generate shadows. Consult your manual to stay in the proper range for the flash to be effective, move your subject away from walls, or angle and "bounce" the flash off of a ceiling or reflector if possible.

ISO

The film speed indicates its sensitivity to light. The higher the ISO, the more sensitive the film (or sensor on a digital camera) is to light. Choosing a higher ISO will achieve better results in low lighting conditions.

WHITE BALANCE

Digital cameras have an added setting—"white balance," the process of removing unrealistic color casts, allowing what looks white in person to appear white in your picture. The camera locates a reference point that represents white to calculate other colors based on it. Most have an automatic white balance setting, while SLRs have additional choices, like cloudy, direct sunlight or incandescent, and the ability to set a custom white balance.

composition

How you compose a photo helps direct the viewer's eye to the focal point—the subject of your image. Keep these guidelines in mind:

EXAMINE THE BACKGROUND

Is there anything near your subject that will detract from it? Is the subject standing in front of any poles, branches or fixtures that will appear to be "growing" out of his head? Eliminate a problematic background by shooting from a different angle, zooming in or relocating the subject.

GET CLOSER

Fill the frame with the most vital object and don't worry about squeezing in all of the surroundings. If your camera doesn't have a zoom lens, zoom with your feet, taking a step or two closer to your subject.

EXPERIMENT WITH WHERE YOU PLACE YOUR SUBJECT

Vary the position of your subject to add interest to each photo. Try this: Follow the "rule of thirds"—divide the viewfinder into thirds horizontally and vertically, creating nine squares. Place your subject in a place where the lines of the squares would intersect. If your camera doesn't allow you to select different focus points, you'll need to center your subject, press the shutter halfway, then recompose your shot.

SEE EYE TO EYE

If you want to make a subject's eyes and expression the focus of your photo, take pictures at eye level. For example, if you're taking a picture of a child, sit or even lie down so you're the same height.

MOVE AROUND

People like different views of their face, and as a photographer you never know what a person is going to like best. Move around and photograph your subject from a variety of angles; even turning the subject's face just a few inches can give a whole new look to the shot.

TAKE MANY SHOTS

Take a variety of shots so you can feature your subject up close as well as in her surroundings. Years later, you'll appreciate having photos of both your subject and the environment, because both contribute to the story you're trying to capture.

IN DEEP *by Wendy Anderson.* **Supplies** *Cardstock:* WorldWin; *Patterned paper, letter stickers and ribbon:* Making Memories; *Accents:* Marcella by K; *Pen:* Uni-ball Signo, Sanford; *Fonts:* SS Mono and Little Days, Internet.

such

an

amazing

bond

Savanna. Brittney. Skyler. Jake. The trouble you four can get into is only matched by how much fun you manage to squeeze into each day. Sure, disagreements happen, rivalry is inevitable, but nothing is stronger than your love for each other. Born just a year apart, you are more like brothers and sisters. And let me tell you, it's a privilege to witness such an amazing bond. 07.07

AMAGING BOND *by Deena Wuest.* **Supplies** *Software:* Adobe Photoshop 4.0, Adobe Systems; *Digital page template:* Tortuga Template No. 35 by Kellie Mize, *www.designerdigitals.com*; *Digital patterned paper:* Sea Salt Paper Pack by Katie Pertiet, *www.designerdigitals.com*; *Fonts:* Avant Garde and Garamond, Internet.

TAKING GREAT SNAPSHOTS

Not every image will be a perfectly lit, flawlessly composed portrait.
In fact, the majority will most likely be snapshots—photos you capture
in the spur of the moment. But "snapshot" doesn't mean "low quality."
These hints will help:

BE PREPARED

Photo opportunities often come at unexpected moments. If you're still learning, keep your camera on automatic so you don't have to search for the right settings. Charge the batteries. If you don't want to "lug" your SLR around, purchase a point-and-shoot so you'll never be without a camera.

KEEP SHOOTING

Not every picture will be a keeper, so snap lots of shots, especially with digital—just delete what you don't want.

TELL THE STORY

Take photos from the beginning, middle and end of the event. Shoot a variety of pictures, from close-ups to group shots to surroundings. Hand the camera to someone else so you can get in some photos, too.

TRY A NEW ANGLE

Play with the angles, especially if you're using a point-and-shoot that controls everything else. Turn the camera vertically, walk around to test different viewpoints, sit on the ground to look up at your subject, climb high to shoot from above or tilt the camera slightly for a dynamic image.

candids

Your subjects' personalities will shine through when they don't pose or put
on "cheesy" smiles. How can you take more natural portraits?

SEE WHAT HAPPENS

Give your subjects something to do, then wait and watch. Have them interact with a pet, share a story or study an object, for example.

KEEP YOUR DISTANCE

If you stand back, the subject will eventually lose interest in you and your camera. Use your zoom lens to get close without being a distraction.

DON'T SMILE FOR THE CAMERA

You don't always have to instruct your subjects to "say cheese!" Snap pictures of loved ones' trademark facial expressions instead.

EXPERT Q&A
with candice stringham

After sharing her tips on important camera features and the advantages of going digital, expert Candice Stringham shares more advice about some common photography dilemmas.

q What about reducing glare and getting true colors in snow shots?

a Reduce dark subjects or gray-colored snow by metering on your subject. Move in and press the shutter halfway, noting what the camera is telling you about the aperture and shutter speed. Set your camera to those settings (or set the "AE Lock" if your SLR has one) and then move back to take the shot.

With a point-and-shoot, you have fewer alternatives. The best practice is to move closer to your subject and cut out the bright sky and as much snow as possible, giving your camera a chance to meter on the subject.

BEFORE

Dark subject in snow.

AFTER

Move closer and meter on subject.

q What about low-light situations, such as school assemblies, museums, plays or recitals?

a In these situations, your flash will rarely help—it has a limited range, typically about 15 feet. If you have a point-and-shoot, you don't have many options, so attempt to sit within 15 feet of the stage (or your subject), and use your flash with the zoom end of your lens.

With an SLR, you'll need a zoom or telephoto lens with a good open aperture of 1.8 or 2.8 so it can let in a lot of light. These lenses may be costly, but if you have children who participate in a lot of activities, it's a good investment. When you're ready to shoot, you'll want to make a few adjustments to your settings:

RAISE THE ISO
The higher the number, the less light you'll need. Learn how to change the setting—an ISO of 800 is good for taking photos in a gym.

ADJUST THE WHITE BALANCE
Change the white balance to obtain better color without an orange or green cast. If you're in a gym, you'll probably use the "fluorescent" setting, while you'll most likely choose "tungsten" in a theater.

OPEN THE APERTURE
Use a low-number aperture, like 1.8 or 2.8 to let in more light. This aperture will also blur the background, keeping your subject in focus.

Adjust camera settings and move closer to subjects in low-light situations.

EXPERT Q&A continued
with candice stringham

q What advice can you give for taking photos with the sun directly above or behind the subject?

a There are several options when working with harsh lighting:

❶ LOOK FOR OPEN SHADE
Anywhere that the light is blocked overhead and open on the sides—like under a large tree—will produce soft light without looking flat.

❷ SHOOT FROM ABOVE
Prevent shadows by having the subject tilt his head up, then shoot from above. If the sun is bright, have him look down until the last second so you can take the picture before he starts to squint.

❸ USE A FILL FLASH
Your camera's flash or fill flash will eliminate the harsh shadows on sunny days.

❹ PLACE YOUR SUBJECT IN FRONT OF THE SUN
Move your subject to prevent squinting. If you're using an SLR, meter on the subject's face, set the AE (auto exposure) lock, step back and shoot.

BEFORE

In harsh light

AFTER

1 Look for open shade.

2 Shoot from above.

3 Use a fill flash.

4 Place subject in front of sun.

journaling

Have you ever looked at a group photo from your childhood and asked, "Who is that, again?" Then you understand the value of adding text to your layouts, otherwise known as "journaling." If pictures are the heart of our pages, journaling is certainly the soul. In this chapter, we'll discuss how your writing can pick up where your images leave off to give future generations the "whole story."

SHARING THE STORY

Journaling gives you the opportunity to record facts and feelings that
might otherwise be forgotten. Carry a small notebook or use your planner
to note details, quotes and moments as they take place. At the very least,
jot down the basics for the photos you've just taken, including:

WHO

Identify the people who can be seen clearly in the photos.
Sure, you may know who everyone is, but future generations may not. For those not in your immediate family, note
their full names and relationships to you.

WHAT

Discuss the activity taking place. What's the occasion?
Why is the moment so funny, poignant or significant?
Why do you want to remember it?

WHEN

Include at least the month and year that the photos were
taken. Although you think you'll remember the date, you
probably won't. It may even be difficult to distinguish
one batch of Christmas photos from another after a few
years pass!

WHERE

Describe where the photos were taken. Include the city
and state or the specific address, especially if it's a place
you visit frequently. Wouldn't you love to see if your grandparents' favorite hangouts are still around?

WHY

Think about details you can add to the page that will reveal
the story behind the story, often the most enjoyable part of
journaling for readers. Why is your daughter smiling? Why
did you vacation here? Why is this your favorite dish?

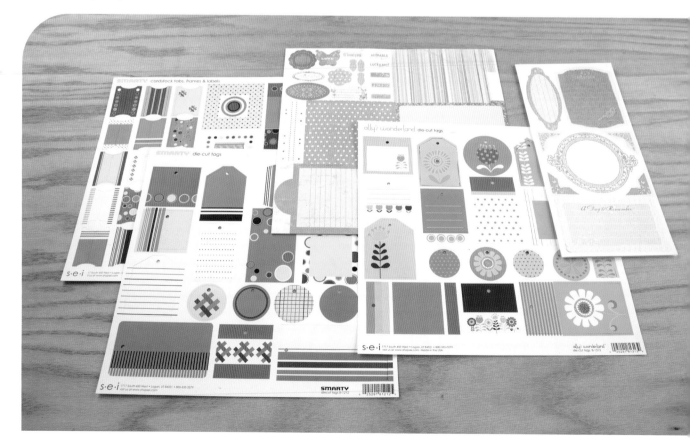

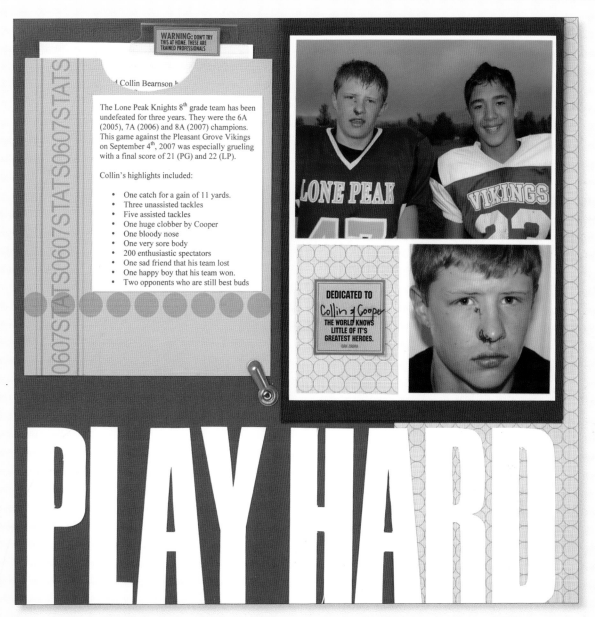

WARNING: DON'T TRY THIS AT HOME. THESE ARE TRAINED PROFESSIONALS

Collin Bearnson

The Lone Peak Knights 8th grade team has been undefeated for three years. They were the 6A (2005), 7A (2006) and 8A (2007) champions. This game against the Pleasant Grove Vikings on September 4th, 2007 was especially grueling with a final score of 21 (PG) and 22 (LP).

Collin's highlights included:

- One catch for a gain of 11 yards.
- Three unassisted tackles
- Five assisted tackles
- One huge clobber by Cooper
- One bloody nose
- One very sore body
- 200 enthusiastic spectators
- One sad friend that his team lost
- One happy boy that his team won.
- Two opponents who are still best buds

DEDICATED TO
Collin & Cooper
THE WORLD KNOWS LITTLE OF IT'S GREATEST HEROES.
DAN ZADRA

PLAY HARD

PLAY HARD by Lisa Bearnson. **Supplies** Software: Adobe Illustrator, Adobe Systems (to create "Stats" strip); Patterned paper: Chatterbox; Letter die cuts: Silhouette, QuicKutz; Photo anchors and quote sticker: 7gypsies; Font: Arial Narrow, Microsoft.

add meaning

Although recording the "who, what and where" is better than nothing at all, most of your stories should go beyond the basics. Whether they're embarrassing or funny, touching or tragic, they're part of your family history—don't be afraid to document them. Writing meaningful journaling isn't as hard as you think if you keep a few simple guidelines in mind:

RECORD THE BEFORE AND AFTER
Allow your text to fill in what your photos don't show. Describe the moment before or after the shutter clicked.

CAPTURE BEHIND THE SCENES
Include one "behind the scenes" incident in your description—something only you would know. Take yourself back to the moment to uncover what you may have forgotten.

CONDUCT INTERVIEWS
Ask family members for their impressions—they may unearth something even you don't remember. Quotes from friends and family members, along with their fresh perspectives, will add richness and variety to your album.

INCLUDE THE DETAILS
Don't hold back your feelings because you think they're "obvious." Consider what future generations will want to discover. If you were leafing through one of your grandparents' scrapbooks, what would you love to learn?

WRITE AND REWRITE
Write a first draft and let some time pass before re-reading. If it doesn't make sense or if you're continually adding details in your mind, revise it.

writing style

As you're composing the journaling for different layouts within the same album, consider why you're creating these pages and to whom you're speaking. That will help answer many of the questions you have about how to write your journaling. Try these ideas:

WRITE THE STORY AS YOU WOULD TELL IT
If you were showing the photos to a friend, would you be talking about them in the past or present tense? Present tense is ideal when you're describing someone's personality or favorites. Past is a good choice if you're recounting previous events.

CONSIDER THE PURPOSE OF YOUR LAYOUT
If you're recording memories for your child, talk to him directly. If your layouts are part of a visual journal, address yourself! For a consistent voice, however, just describe the events and emotions as they occurred.

CONSIDER THE AUDIENCE
Cater journaling to each batch of photos, just like you do with the design. Writing in the third person lets you serve as the "narrator." If you'd rather contribute your feelings and impressions, opt for the first person. Present facts objectively on heritage pages (if you weren't there and don't "know" the subject), for example, or from your own point of view if you're describing a trip to the park with your daughter.

will she ever **forgive** me?

As sisters growing up together, we have a lot of life stories, some worth sharing, some not, some unforgettable, and some so forgettable, I can't remember them happening at all. And then there are some stories that get dragged up again and again. Like the time I convinced Kylene to crawl into the dog's house (that hadn't been used in, oh...ever). It's a story that she will never let me forget. She loves to tell how I laughed and laughed when she came running out of the house, screaming in terror of the wasps who were stinging every exposed inch of her skin. You see, what none of us knew, when we convinced Kylene to play doggie, was that a family of wasps had built their nest in the doghouse, and those baby wasps were about to hatch. So Kylene committed the worst crime in wasp-society possible: she threatened their babies. And what do I have to say for my own part in this? Did I really laugh at her terror, at her pain? Yes, I'm afraid I did, and it wasn't the first, nor the last time either. I have since learned that laughing is my response to fear. It is a reflex and completely uncontrollable. So when Sean and I talked Kylene into being a dog and using the doghouse, and the family of wasps with their nest full of babies stung her and stung her and stung her, and I laughed and laughed, it wasn't because I am a cruel and uncaring sister, it was because I was scared myself. That's the truth. If you spend enough time with us, you'll certainly hear the story at least once, and then you can decide for yourself, whether you believe me or not. As for Kylene?
All she remembers is her big sister laughing at her pain...Will she ever forgive me?

Kylene's favorite story since ca. 1981

FORGIVE by Amber Ries. **Supplies** *Software:* Adobe Photoshop CS2, Adobe Systems; *Digital paper:* Krafty Elegance Paper Pack (brown), Perfect Pets Paper Pack (orange and stripe) and Puzzled Paper Pack (green and red) by Katie Pertiet, *www.designerdigitals.com*; *Digital stitches:* Digital Stitches Brown by Katie Pertiet, *www.designerdigitals.com*; *Digital frames:* Krafty Photo Frames No. 2 by Katie Pertiet, *www.designerdigitals.com*; *Digital corrugated letters:* Out-of-a-Box Alphabet by Katie Pertiet, *www.designerdigitals.com*; *Digital magazine-cut letters:* Little Bits Alphabet by Katie Pertiet, *www.designerdigitals.com*; *Digital felt accents:* Felt Board Friends Bee-autiful Blooms by Pattie Knox, *www.designerdigitals.com*; *Digital doghouse sticker:* Doggone Cute Stickers by Mindy Terasawa, *www.designerdigitals.com*; *Digital notebook paper and label:* Falling for You by Gina Cabrera, *www.digitaldesignessentials.com*; *Fonts:* Palatino Linotype and Times New Roman, Microsoft.

1) A great reader
2) A very messy eater
3) Dress like a Tomboy
4) Love to go shopping

5) A noisy sleeper - snore!
6) Love to have play dates
7) Like to watch Sponge Bob
8) Shy until you know someone
9) cuddly and lovable

THE WAY YOU ARE AT 8 by Suzy Plantamura. **Supplies** *Cardstock:* Bazzill Basics Paper and Prism Papers; *Patterned paper, velvet paper and letter stickers:* SEI; *Epoxy flowers and ribbon:* KI Memories; *Felt flower and circle:* Maya Road; *Pen:* EK Success.

BATTLING WRITER'S BLOCK

A blank page can be intimidating, even if you're writing about the people you love and the events you've experienced. If you've been staring at the background for several minutes, you can break the block with a few simple exercises:

GO BACK
Mentally return to the moment you took the picture. What made you pick up the camera in the first place? What were you and your subject feeling?

BRAINSTORM
Pick up some scrap paper and write about your photos—without stopping or editing—for 5–10 minutes. Let whatever flows from your pen become the foundation for your journaling.

TALK IT OUT
Chat with friends or family about the event—the discussion may help you discover what was truly significant about the moment.

FIND OTHER SOURCES
Maybe you've already got text for your page. Check your journal, e-mails, blog or planner. Is there something you can cut and paste or turn into simple list journaling? Or let someone else do the talking—search for a famous quote or song lyric that might adequately express your emotions.

DON'T WORRY
If you're afraid to write because you think the story will be too boring, silly or sappy, stop worrying. These are your albums; don't worry what anyone else will think. Say what you feel.

ADD IT LATER
Eliminate the pressure of the blank spot. Turn a photo into a pocket or add an envelope where you can add journaling when it comes to you.

TAKE A BREAK
Set the layout aside and move onto something else. Trying to "force" your journaling will only frustrate you or result in the generic, "We had a fun day at the park." Trust that the words will come to you eventually.

DESIGN

You thought out the content, now brainstorm the style. Find inspiration for the look of your journaling in magazines, on billboards, on product packaging and from other layouts. The method you choose can affect the page's feel, tone and the time it takes to create it. Think about these options:

HANDWRITING

Journaling longhand adds a personal touch. Test the length on scrap paper. You can write in pencil and trace with pen to avoid mistakes. If you're self-conscious about your penmanship, don't be. Wouldn't you love an album filled with your grandmother's writing, regardless of what it looks like?

COMPUTER FONTS

If you prefer a uniform feel, type and print your journaling. You can easily make the style match your page with the huge variety of fonts available.

STICKERS

Using stickers to complete anything other than captions can be time-consuming. To adhere them straight, either draw light pencil lines that can be erased later or tack the bottom edge of the stickers to the top edge of a ruler, press the tops onto the page, then remove the ruler.

STAMPS OR RUB-ONS

Additional planning goes into using stamps and rub-ons since you can't move them like stickers. Use a stamp positioner for perfectly aligned letters, or cut and arrange rub-ons to ensure perfect spacing.

COMBINATION JOURNALING

Get creative with your supplies and create your journaling by combining your favorite supplies . . . perhaps handwriting with computer fonts or stickers with rub-ons. It takes a little extra planning but can add lots of punch to a page.

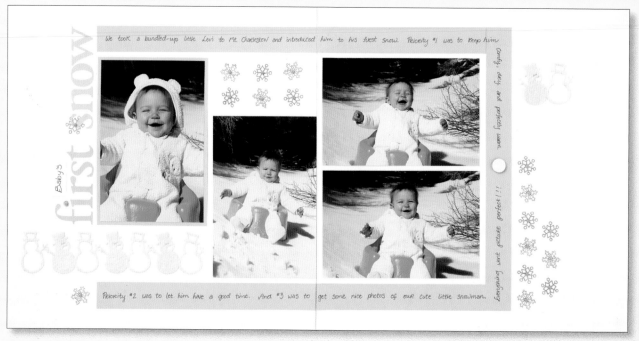

BABY'S FIRST SNOW by Leah LaMontagne. **Supplies** Cardstock: Bazzill Basics; Patterned paper: SEI; Stamps, felt snowmen and brads: Queen & Co.; Letter die cuts: Cricut, Provo Craft; Ink: Stampin' Up!; Pen: Zig Writer, EK Success.

journaling style

Getting creative with your journaling is half the fun. That said, just be sure it's still legible and has as much visual weight as the photos by using some classic journaling styles:

BLOCKS

Writing in paragraph form is the easiest way to recount a long story or discuss a serious subject that wouldn't suit a "whimsical" style. Create text in a column or square, directly on the background or on an item you can add to it.

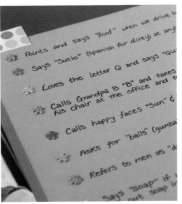

LISTS

Turn event highlights, an inventory of favorites or a catalog of qualities into a journaling list. Add text to the background using brads, gems or other small accents as "bullets," or write lines on strips of cardstock to add interest.

SHAPES

For a playful look, handwrite or use photo-editing software or WordArt in Microsoft Word to format journaling into shapes like ovals or circles. Avoid detailed shapes that make your text difficult to read.

BORDERS

Journaling can pull double duty as a border or frame. Limit it to brief text—your reader will tire of turning the album to read a long story.

LAYERS

Layer text over the background of a large photo or a scenic image. Add it with photo-editing software before printing or with rub-ons or stamps after. (Have duplicates on hand if you're concerned about mistakes or the long-term effects.)

POCKETS

To keep journaling private, "hide" it in a pocket (adhere a photo or piece of cardstock along three edges, leaving one open to insert journaling), in an envelope or beneath a flap. It's perfect if you want to finish the page now but add text later.

JOURNALING PROMPTS

If all of your journaling comes from your perspective, you're only recording one side of every tale. Vary the viewpoints—from time to time, show a family member an incomplete layout and have her add the text. Or create layouts around "interviews" you've conducted with her. Stumped for topics? Try one of the following:

CHILDHOOD

- What are/were your favorite games and toys?
- Discuss a time you got into trouble. What was your punishment?
- What subjects did you enjoy in school?
- Have you ever had a nickname? How did you get it?
- Describe a teacher or role model you admired.

FAMILY AND FRIENDS

- Name one of your mother's or father's qualities you wish to emulate.
- What do you remember about your grandparents?
- Discuss what you like and dislike most about your siblings.
- How did you meet your best friend? Why do you enjoy spending time with him or her?
- Describe your family pet.

FEELINGS

- What's the scariest thing that's ever happened to you?
- Reveal your most embarrassing moment.
- Name something you've done or said that you wish you could take back.
- What are your pet peeves?
- Describe your dream day.

FAVORITES

- Describe one meal that you could eat every day.
- Relive your most memorable vacation. What activities did you enjoy?
- Do you have any birthday traditions? What's the best gift you've ever received?
- What holiday do you look forward to and why?
- Discuss your favorite time of day.

ACCOMPLISHMENTS

- Name your biggest achievement.
- Discuss a goal you set for yourself and how you reached it.
- Describe a moment in which you surprised even yourself.
- What was your first job? What did you like and dislike about it?
- What do you want to be when you grow up?

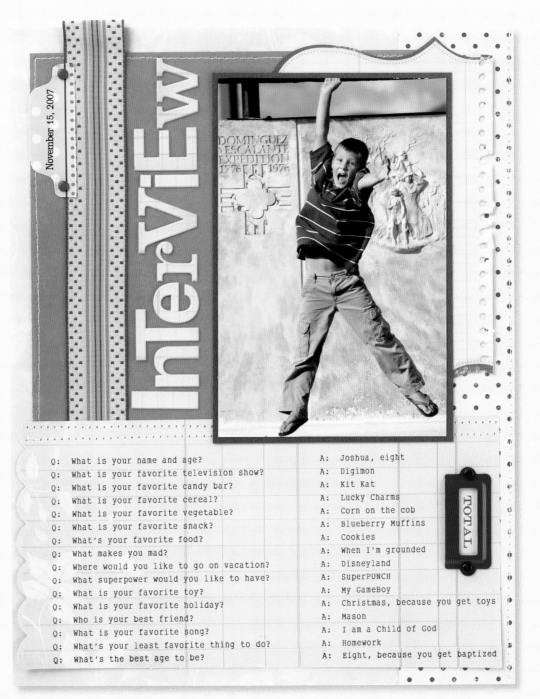

November 15, 2007

InTerVIEw

Q:	What is your name and age?	A:	Joshua, eight
Q:	What is your favorite television show?	A:	Digimon
Q:	What is your favorite candy bar?	A:	Kit Kat
Q:	What is your favorite cereal?	A:	Lucky Charms
Q:	What is your favorite vegetable?	A:	Corn on the cob
Q:	What is your favorite snack?	A:	Blueberry Muffins
Q:	What's your favorite food?	A:	Cookies
Q:	What makes you mad?	A:	When I'm grounded
Q:	Where would you like to go on vacation?	A:	Disneyland
Q:	What superpower would you like to have?	A:	SuperPUNCH
Q:	What is your favorite toy?	A:	My GameBoy
Q:	What is your favorite holiday?	A:	Christmas, because you get toys
Q:	Who is your best friend?	A:	Mason
Q:	What is your favorite song?	A:	I am a Child of God
Q:	What's your least favorite thing to do?	A:	Homework
Q:	What's the best age to be?	A:	Eight, because you get baptized

TOTAL

INTERVIEW *by Wendy Anderson.* **Supplies** *Patterned paper, letters and ribbon:* Making Memories; *Bookplate:* Art Warehouse, Creative Imaginations; *Brads:* Doodlebug Design; *Tab punch:* McGill; *Font:* Small Type Writing, Internet.

9

digital scrapbooking

If you've ever typed and printed journaling for a layout or corrected a photo before printing it out, you've essentially dabbled in the world of digital scrapbooking. What is digital scrapbooking? It's selecting photos, choosing backgrounds, adding journaling, creating embellishments . . . all on your computer. If you'd like to design an entire page without leaving your desk, discover what it'll take to get started.

WHAT YOU'LL NEED

Digital scrapbooking has its equivalent of a paper trimmer, adhesives, templates and pens all rolled into one—a computer. If you edit and print your own photos, you may already have everything you need to create a digital page. Consult this checklist to be sure:

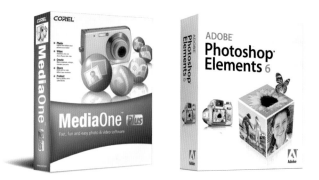

HARDWARE AND SOFTWARE

Digital scrapbooking will require a computer and some graphics or photo-editing software, like Adobe Photoshop Elements, Adobe Photoshop CS3, Corel PaintShop Pro or Microsoft Digital Image Pro. Familiarize yourself with your software by studying the tutorial.

PHOTOS

You'll need digital photos or a scanner to get printed photos into your system.

DIGITAL SUPPLIES

As with traditional scrapbooking, digital comes with its own supplies. If you're just experimenting, find digital "freebies" through a search on the Internet. To complete your first page, you'll need at least one sheet of digital patterned paper (it'll be a .jpg file) and a few embellishments (.png files, which you can open in your software and drag onto your document).

PRINTER

You'll probably want to print your layouts. Pages larger than 8½" x 11" will require a large-format printer unless you want to reduce them to 8" x 8". Numerous online photo-developing services will print 12" x 12".

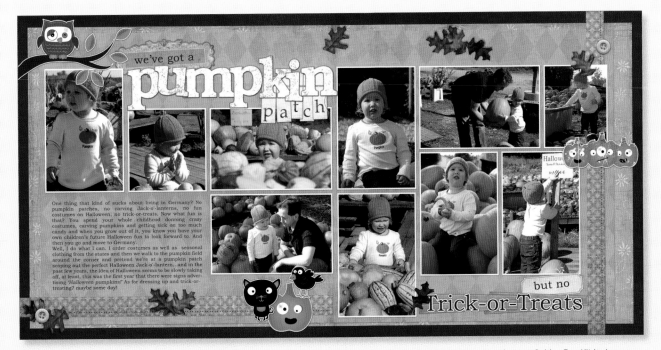

WE'VE GOT A PUMPKIN PATCH by Amber Ries. **Supplies** *Software:* Adobe Photoshop CS2, Adobe Systems; *Digital patterned paper:* Golden Boy Kit by Lynn Grieveson, *www.designerdigitals.com;* Autumn Harvest Paper Pack (floral) by Katie Pertiet, *www.designerdigitals.com; Digital chipboard letters:* Chunky White Chipboard Alphabet by Katie Pertiet, *www.designerdigitals.com; Digital letter strips:* Alphabet Strips by Katie Pertiet, *www.designerdigitals.com; Digital leaves:* Little Paper Leaves by Katie Pertiet, *www.designerdigitals.com; Digital drop shadows:* Drop Shadow Action Set by Katie Pertiet, *www.designerdigitals.com; Digital stickers:* Little Creepers by Mindy Terasawa, *www.designerdigitals.com; Digital paper (green), buttons, ribbon, stitching, title block and title strips:* Harvest Spice, *www.shabbyprincess.com; Digital title block:* Jubilant Kit by Gina Cabrera, *www.digitaldesignessentials.com; Font:* Bookman Old Style, Internet.

DID YOU NOTICE?

Whether you're creating a traditional scrapbook page with your supplies or a digital
page with digital elements, call attention to your title by combining different lettering styles.

WHAT YOU'LL WANT

Once you've got the basics down, you'll want to expand your digital stash to include a few extras:

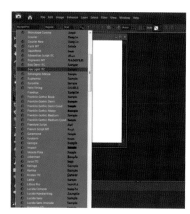

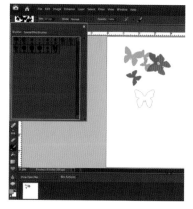

FONTS

Turn to them for titles, journaling, captions and other text effects.

BRUSHES

A brush is like a digital version of a rubber stamp—a simple way to add flourishes and designs to photos and backgrounds.

KITS

Most digital designers create kits—inexpensive, coordinating packages of digital patterned paper, Photoshop brushes, journaling spots, ribbon and other embellishments. Smaller packages of journaling blocks, flourish stamps or photo frames, for example, are also available. As an added bonus, you never use up digital supplies, making them highly economical.

EQUIPMENT

If you fall in love with digital, you may want to invest in additional accessories, such as an external hard drive to store digital layouts and supplies, an organizational program such as ACDSee Photo Manager to organize your files, or even a pen tablet to add doodles or handwriting directly to your pages.

interior design
scrapbooking's first cousin

Before I discovered the world of scrapbooking, I spent hours upon hours studying home decor, watching HGTV and Christopher Lowell, and decorating our (obviously) 60s style home. I loved picking out colors and devising a plan for the overall feel of a space. Before I knew it, I had created an entire book of ideas I wanted to bring to fruition, but no more rooms in our house to experiment with.

Enter digital scrapbooking. I was in pure heaven. I could use all the same basic design principles, color combinations, and move my designs around without breaking my back! And the best part...if an idea didn't turn out like I pictured, I could just hit UNDO (gotta love that undo button). That definitely doesn't work with home decor. Just ask the five coats of paint on my bathroom walls!

I find now after scrapbooking for almost six years that designing a space in our home is much more fun and rewarding. I believe that I will always have a passion for interior design. However, my first love remains firmly in scrapbooking. Long after paint peels and walls crumble, my family will have these albums, these love notes to read and know how much they are loved. No can of paint could ever do that.

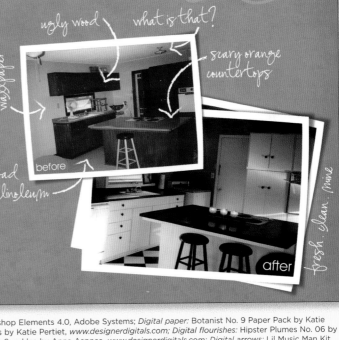

ugly wood

what is that?

scary orange countertops

floral wallpaper

before

bad linoleum

fresh. clean. mine

after

INTERIOR DESIGN by Deena Wuest. **Supplies** *Software:* Adobe Photoshop Elements 4.0, Adobe Systems; *Digital paper:* Botanist No. 9 Paper Pack by Katie Pertiet, *www.designerdigitals.com; Digital frames:* Curled Photo Frames by Katie Pertiet, *www.designerdigitals.com; Digital flourishes:* Hipster Plumes No. 06 by Anna Aspnes, *www.designerdigitals.com; Digital sparkle accents:* Magic Sparkles by Anna Aspnes, *www.designerdigitals.com; Digital arrows:* Lil Music Man Kit by Mindy Terasawa, *www.designerdigitals.com; Fonts:* Avant Garde and Susie's Hand, Internet.

HIDDEN GEMS *by Kimber McGray.* **Supplies** *Software:* Adobe Photoshop Elements 3.0, Adobe Systems; *All digital elements:* ReFRESHing Kit, *www.polkadot-potato.com; Font:* Chantilly-Medium, Internet.

DID YOU NOTICE?

Kimber drew inspiration from her photos when she chose the red
and yellow papers for her layout.

WHAT TO DO WITH DIGITAL LAYOUTS

There's one question many paper scrapbookers ask about digital: What do you do with the pages once they're done? If you think your digi layouts will stagnate on your hard drive, think again:

PRINT AND DISPLAY
Print completed pages and slip them into page protectors just as you would traditional layouts. If you create albums for each family member, this will save you time; instead of designing several versions of the same event, simply print multiple copies of the same layout.

MINI ALBUMS
Print layouts in different sizes for use in full-size albums, mini books or even tiny photo charms.

BOUND BOOKS
Use a photo lab or online developer to print and bind your pages into a hardback book—the perfect present for family and friends.

SCREEN SAVER
Store layouts on your hard drive and run them as a slideshow screen saver of your recent or favorite work.

GIFT CD
Burn layouts onto compact discs to send to family and friends.

E-MAIL
E-mail digital pages to family members to share.

BASIC HOW-TO

Though specific instructions and commands vary depending on your particular software application, there are a handful of fundamental steps you'll need to follow to design digitally. I asked digital expert Jessica Sprague to explain the "bare bones" process to provide the general idea.

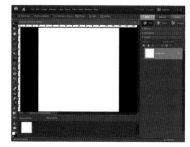

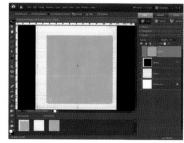

❶ OPEN A NEW DOCUMENT
To create a digital page, open a blank document in your graphics program. I recommend Adobe Photoshop Elements—it strikes a good balance between user-friendliness and creative options. It's reasonably priced, and you can learn to use most basic features in a few weeks. Also, because the user community is very large, most digital tutorials are written for Photoshop Elements, and it's the most compatible with digital kits.

❷ ADD DIGITAL PAPERS
Add in your digital patterned-paper background. This usually involves opening the patterned-paper file and dragging the paper onto your new layout document.

❸ ADD PHOTOS
Locate the desired photos on your hard drive, open them and add them to your page. If you want to scrapbook printed photos, you'll need to scan and save them onto your computer first.

❹ EMBELLISH
Add journaling, a title and embellishments, as desired.

❺ PRINT
Print your layout or save the file as a .jpg so you can upload it to your online photo developer or take it to a local shop that prints 12″ x 12″ pages.

this → (ice cream grin)

makes me happy.

I get much more pleasure out of watching you eat your sweet ice cream cone than even tasting one myself.

CAPTURED BY MOM

And that is saying something.

2

THIS MAKES ME HAPPY *by Jessica Sprague.* **Supplies** *Software:* Adobe Photoshop CS3, Adobe Systems; *Digital paper:* Peachy Keen Kit (stripe) by Rhonna Farrer, *www.twopeasinabucket.com*; *Digital frame:* Split Pea Kit by Rhonna Farrer, *www.twopeasinabucket.com*; *Digital paper:* Illuminated-Enlightened Paper Add-On (blue) by Jen Wilson, *www.jenwilsondesigns.com*; *Digital scalloped border:* Festival, *www.shabbyprincess.com*; *Digital scallop paper mask:* Border Templates by Katie Pertiet, *www.designerdigitals.com*; *Digital negative frame:* Storyboard Negatives by Katie Pertiet, *www.designerdigitals.com*; *Digital letters:* Botanist Notebook No. 1 Kit by Katie Pertiet, *www.designerdigitals.com*; *Digital circle date:* Digital Date Stamps Vol. 4 by Katie Pertiet, *www.designerdigitals.com*; *Fonts:* Ma Sexy, *www.dafont.com*; Palatino Linotype, Microsoft.

EXPERT Q&A
with jessica sprague

Beyond the basics of creating a digital scrapbook page, what else should you know? I asked Jessica to share more insights about this exciting new aspect of scrapbooking. Learn why she loves the tech-driven side of the craft—and discover a few of her design tips, too.

q What are the advantages of digital scrapbooking?

a I love paper scrapbooking. I love digital scrapbooking. I think each has enormous creative possibilities. What I love most are the options I get from knowing how to do both and the freedom of being able to mix and match. Digital opens up so many fantastic possibilities, including:

A CHALLENGE
Digital scrapbooking is not necessarily easy to master, but challenging yourself to learn something completely new can be exciting!

SPEED
I recently created an entire 20-page album for my husband in a single afternoon. I simply used a premade page background available in Adobe Photoshop Elements, added a few touches of my own (including his photos and journaling), and uploaded it to an online developer all within a few hours.

SUPPLIES
Roaming the virtual aisles of an online digital shop gives me the same creative boost as walking through my local scrapbook store. Plus, you can store an entire room full of digital scrapbook supplies on an external hard drive the size of a paperback book.

CLEANUP
Cleanup from digital scrapbooking is as simple as closing the lid of your laptop or turning off your monitor and walking away. And you can come back to it just as easily—all of your work is preserved on the computer.

FLEXIBILITY
One comment I hear from paper scrapbookers is that they're too "hands-on" to try a digital page. That's why I love "hybrid" scrapbooking—I can incorporate a few computer tricks (like adding swirls to photos, creating photo collages, typing titles or even downloading clip art for use as embellishments) onto paper layouts and have the best of both worlds.

q What are a few of your favorite digital design tricks?

a To create visual interest, I love using textured patterned papers as my backgrounds. I usually line up my photos or group them in a grid, which lends a clean look to the page. I love to add photo frames or swirl brushes around the edges of my photos, then use fonts to complete the look.

(ice cream grin)

q What's the one piece of advice you'd give to a new digital scrapbooker?

a Take an online class, walk through a tutorial or two, familiarize yourself with the basic techniques involved, and you'll be amazed what you can create.

5 weeks

first smile caught on film

09.27.07

initial
communication

There was nothing in the world that could have prepared me for your first smile. Your dad and I were standing in the kitchen talking to you when you spontaneously erupted in a huge grin. A grin so huge that it made your nose wrinkle. A grin so huge that it made your eyes absolutely light up. It was a moment I'll never forget. You. Communicating. With us. For the first time.

INITIAL COMMUNICATION *by Deena Wuest.* **Supplies** *Software:* Adobe Photoshop Elements 4.0, Adobe Systems; *Digital shapes:* Frame It Custom Shapes by Anna Aspnes, *www.designerdigitals.com*; *Digital brushes:* Freshly Worn Photo Brushes-n-Overlays by Katie Pertiet, *www.designerdigitals.com*; *Digital frame:* Dried Brush Frames by Katie Pertiet, *www.designerdigitals.com*; *Fonts:* Avant Garde, Hannibal Lecter and Impact, Internet.

DID YOU NOTICE?

Make a big impact on your layout by featuring a photo enlargement.

Deena used the extra space on her photo to add journaling.

inspiration

Of all the ways to gather page ideas, looking at other scrapbookers' layouts has to be my favorite. They can be used as page sketches, as theme prompts or as pure design inspiration. Look beyond a layout's subject to study its color scheme, photography style, accents, title, texture and technique. Fill your creative well with the following examples. Apply the concepts directly to your pages or use them as a springboard for more ideas.

BABIES

Adorable. Amazing. Always changing. A new baby is the reason most of us started scrapbooking—it provides the chance to record every moment and milestone. From snoozing and smiling to exploring and cooing, there's an abundance of scrapworthy occasions to choose from.

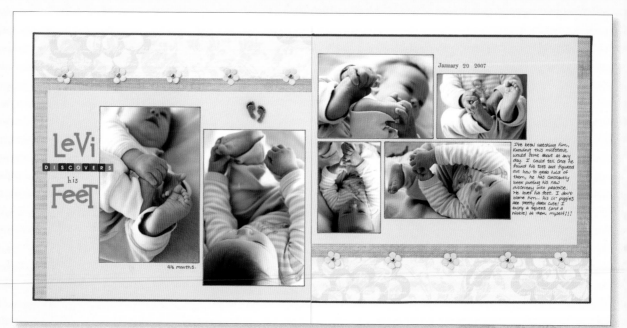

LEVI DISCOVERS HIS FEET *by Leah LaMontagne.* **Supplies** *Cardstock:* Prism Papers; *Patterned paper:* Fancy Pants Designs and Scenic Route; *Letter stickers:* All My Memories and KI Memories; *Letter stamps:* Hero Arts; *Date stamp:* Technique Tuesday; *Ink:* Stampin' Up!; *Charms and brads:* Making Memories; *Pens:* Zig Writer, EK Success.

DID YOU NOTICE?

Leah used brads to decorate the flowers on her layout.

MOMMY & BABY: AMBER & DEAN: MOTHER & SON...

AMBER & DEAN: MOTHER &

NOV 07

November 7th

MAYBE THIS IS HOW IT ALWAYS IS, THAT THE 2ND, 3RD, 4TH CHILD ALWAYS GETS A LITTLE LESS OF MOMMY, A LITTLE LESS OF DADDY. IT'S CERTAINLY NOT WHAT I PLANNED, THOUGH I ADMIT TO WORRYING ABOUT IT FROM DAY 1: THIS WHOLE ADAPTING TO A 2ND CHILD THING. I MEAN, HOW DO YOU GIVE NO. 2 AS MUCH TIME AS YOU WERE ABLE TO GIVE NO. 1? HOW DO YOU MAKE SURE NO. 1 ISN'T FEELING LEFT-OUT, OR REPLACED?

IT IS NOW 5 WEEKS SINCE DEAN APPEARED ON THE SCENE AND I STILL DON'T HAVE THE ANSWERS TO THOSE QUESTIONS. WE GO DAY BY DAY, DOING OUR BEST TO MAKE SURE GEORGIA DOESN'T FEEL NEGLECTED, OFTEN CAUSING DEAN TO BE LEFT TO CRY MUCH LONGER THAN WE EVER WOULD HAVE LEFT GEORGIA, AND I HOPE FOR MOMENTS LIKE THESE: MOMENTS WHERE I CAN CUDDLE WITH DEAN, BREATHE IN HIS SCENT (WHICH IS PREDOMINANTLY THAT OF SPIT-UP FROM MY LITTLE SPIT-UP KING) AND FEEL HIS VELVET-SOFT SKIN. TO HAVE A MOMENT THAT IS SOLELY AND COMPLETELY OURS, WHERE EXHAUSTION AND HEARTACHE IS FORGOTTEN, JUST THIS ONE MOMENT, THE TWO OF US, BEFORE HE IS TOO BIG TO CUDDLE FROM CHIN TO TUMMY, AND TOO WRIGGLY TO FALL ASLEEP IN MY ARMS. JUST THIS ONE MOMENT IN TIME FOR US.

I Love You

JUST ONE moment

JUST ONE MOMENT by Amber Ries. **Supplies** *Software:* Adobe Photoshop CS2, Adobe Systems; *Digital paper:* Hom{e}age Page Set by Anna Aspnes, *www.designerdigitals.com*; *Digital flourishes:* Oversize Hipster Plumes No. 1 by Anna Aspnes, *www.designerdigitals.com*; *Digital frame:* Deckled Edge Frames by Katie Pertiet, *www.designerdigitals.com*; *Digital journaling block:* Curled Journal Spots by Katie Pertiet, *www.designerdigitals.com*; *Digital letters:* Chenille Alphabet by Katie Pertiet, *www.designerdigitals.com*; *Digital clock:* Clock Parts No. 2 by Katie Pertiet, *www.designerdigitals.com*; *Digital stitching:* Double Up Stitching No. 1 by Katie Pertiet, *www.designerdigitals.com*; *Digital "I Love You" accent:* Greeting Dots Brushes-n-Stamps by Katie Pertiet, *www.designerdigitals.com*; *Digital drop shadows:* Drop Shadow Action Set by Katie Pertiet, *www.designerdigitals.com*; *Digital ribbon:* Frayed Knots by Lynn Grieveson, *www.designerdigitals.com*; *Digital staples:* Lynn Grieveson, *www.designerdigitals.com*; *Digital date tab:* D&W Tuckables by Kellie Mize, *www.designerdigitals.com*; *Digital flower:* Punched Tags Brushes-n-Stamps by Jesse Edwards, *www.designerdigitals.com*; *Font:* Pupcat, Internet.

Dear Seth,

You were barely two years old yourself, and I don't think you really knew what was happening. I'm sure you didn't understand what having a baby would mean. You didn't realize that you wouldn't be the baby any more. You didn't know you'd be sharing my attention (and affection) with someone else. The fact that Zachary arrived five weeks early meant that you *weren't* the baby five weeks earlier than we had thought. It was hard for you at first, I think. You didn't have anger or aggression toward either of us . . . but at first, you weren't really very interested in the baby either. At the hospital, you didn't want to hold him or be close to him (that's why there aren't pictures of the two of you there). It took a few days...but your curiosity slowly grew and you wanted to know more about this new little baby we had living in our home. You wanted to touch him and talk to him and even kiss him. I was so relieved to see you bonding with him. I know you love him (you loved him before you even realized you did). And do you know what? Just because Zach came along and made you a big brother doesn't mean you can't still be my baby too. I love you so much, and I know you will be a great big brother!

♡ Mommy

BiG brOtheR

BIG BROTHER by *Wendy Anderson.* **Supplies** *Cardstock:* KI Memories; *Patterned paper:* Scenic Route; *Chipboard accents:* American Crafts (star) and O'Scrap! (letters); *Star accents:* Heidi Swapp for Advantus; *Pen and ribbon:* American Crafts; *Brads:* Karen Foster Design; *Font:* SS Mono, www.simplescrapbooksmag.com.

...freedom!

Laura 12/05

GUARANTEED *trouble!*

Laura— You thought you
were hot stuff when you
figured out how the
walker worked. You pushed
your way all around the
house walking so fast to the
point where you lost control!
When you hit a wall, you didn't
turn it around— you just pushed from
the front!
— journaled 11/07

FREEDOM *by Kimber McGray.* **Supplies** *Cardstock:* Bazzill Basics Paper and WorldWin; *Patterned paper:* My Mind's Eye; *Letter stickers and pen:* American Crafts; *Chipboard accent:* Scenic Route; *Brads:* Imaginisce; *Photo turns:* 7gypsies.

DID YOU NOTICE?

You can unify a two-page spread by spreading your title across both pages

edom!

DISCOVERING PLAY *by Deena Wuest.* **Supplies** *Software:* Adobe Photoshop Elements 4.0, Adobe Systems; *Digital paper:* Purely Happy Paper Pack by Katie Pertiet, *www.designerdigitals.com; Fonts:* Avant Garde and Impact, Internet.

DID YOU NOTICE?

Deena creatively placed her photos within her title letters on this digital layout. You can do the same manually: Simply position a large letter template over each image, trace and cut.

DEAN'S SLEEPING HABITS:
FALL 2007

SLEEP LIKE A baby?

YOU KNOW THAT OLD SAYING? THE ONE THAT GOES: I SLEPT LIKE A BABY...? WELL ALL I CAN SAY TO THAT IS: I SURE HOPE NOT! MAN, GETTING A BABY TO SLEEP AT ALL IS A CHALLENGE, AND TO STAY ASLEEP? NO ONE WANTS TO SLEEP LIKE A BABY, NO ONE! I'LL TRY ANYTHING TO GET MY BABY TO SLEEP, EVEN GIVING HIM A PACIFIER, SOMETHING I AM GENERALLY AGAINST. BUT MY BABIES DON'T TAKE PACIFIERS ANYWAY, SO THAT'S ANOTHER ATTEMPT DOWN THE DRAIN. IT'S JUST NOT THAT EASY, STICK A PACIFIER IN BABY'S MOUTH, ROCK BABY GENTLY AND THEN LAY BABY DOWN IN THE CRIB AND WALK AWAY. WHO MADE UP THAT STORY ANYWAY? BECAUSE MY BABIES? THEY NEED OTHER THINGS TO SOOTHE THEM, AND THEY WEREN'T TELLING ME... THEY LEFT IT ALL TO TRIAL AND ERROR

TAKE DEAN: I TRIED NURSING HIM WHILE LYING DOWN SO THAT HE COULD JUST STAY PUT AFTER FALLING ASLEEP - NOPE, HE DOESN'T LIKE NURSING THAT WAY. I TRIED STATIC NOISES, SOMETHING HIS SISTER COULDN'T DO WITHOUT. NO GOOD. I TRIED SWADDLING. SWADDLING ONLY WORKS HALF-WAY, IT CALMS HIM DOWN AND KEEPS HIM FROM STARTLING HIMSELF AWAKE, BUT WON'T KEEP HIM ASLEEP OR PUT HIM TO SLEEP EITHER. I HAVE A CRADLE TO ROCK HIM IN, BUT HE LIES THERE, EYES WIDE OPEN, BEFORE BEGINNING TO FUSS. SO FINALLY, IN DESPAIR, I TRIED THE BABY SWING, AND THAT WAS IT, THE MAGIC TICKET. NOW IF I COULD ONLY GET HIM TO FIGURE OUT NIGHT VS. DAY...

SLEEP LIKE A BABY by Amber Ries. **Supplies** *Software:* Adobe Photoshop CS2, Adobe Systems; *Digital paper:* Night Magic Kit by Lynn Greiveson, *www.designerdigitals.com*; *Digital ribbon:* Island Blues Kit by Lynn Greiveson, *www.designerdigitals.com*; *Digital paper curls:* Curled Paper Edges No. 3 by Anna Aspnes, *www.designerdigitals.com*; *Digital birds:* Something to Crow About by Pattie Knox, *www.designerdigitals.com*; *Digital journaling block:* Curled Notebook Paper by Katie Pertiet, *www.designerdigitals.com*; *Digital ribbon (brown):* Sheridan Kit by Katie Pertiet, *www.designerdigitals.com*; *Digital paper:* Gingham Collection Paper Pack by Katie Pertiet, *www.designerdigitals.com*; *Digital letters:* Chipboard Alphabet by Katie Pertiet, *www.designerdigitals.com*; *Digital stickers and stitching:* Little Flyer Kit by Katie Pertiet, *www.designerdigitals.com*; *Font:* Pea Bailey, Internet.

TODDLERS TO TEENS

In the blink of an eye, your baby grows from toddler to child, child to teen. Document every stage in between with layouts that capture not only their achievements and activities, but the meaningful, everyday moments, too.

These little playmobil horses have become very common around here. You always have one in your hands and you take at least one to bed with you. The playmobil catalogue is your favourite 'book' and all the pages that have horses on them are doggy eared. As your vocabulary begins to grow and develop, your love of horses is very evident. Hee (horse) is heard non stop all day long. When you discovered little playmobil buckets and barrels that could be filled with water for your hees you learned wah-er (water) and grink (drink) and asked incessantly for me to fill them up for you. There are always little tiny puddles throughout the house. Then came sah-oh (saddle) and bry-oh (bridal) and those became your obsession for awhile. You'd take them off and put them back on and exchange them with others from different horses.

I love that you have such a passion for something as wonderful as horses. It seems to grow stronger everyday and you know what, I am really starting to love them too, maybe not as much as you do, though.

July 2007 – 22months

horse hee

HEE *by Amber Ries. Photos by Cara Vincens.* **Supplies** *Software:* Adobe Photoshop CS2, Adobe Systems; *Digital paper:* Spots Dots Paper Pack (blue and yellow) by Katie Pertiet, *www.designerdigitals.com*; Sea Salt Paper Pack (brown) by Katie Pertiet, *www.designerdigitals.com*; Little Birdie Paper Pack (orange) by Katie Pertiet, *www.designerdigitals.com*; *Digital frames:* Round Up Frames Brushes-n-Stamps by Katie Pertiet, *www.designerdigitals.com*; Deckled Edge Frames by Katie Pertiet, *www.designerdigitals.com*; *Digital word strip:* Digital Poetry by Katie Pertiet, *www.designerdigitals.com*; *Digital twine and stars:* Doodled Daydreams Kit by Katie Pertiet, *www.designerdigitals.com*; *Digital drop shadows:* Drop Shadow Action Set by Katie Pertiet, *www.designerdigitals.com*; *Digital felt letters:* Katie's Jewels Felt Alphabet Collection by Pattie Knox, *www.designerdigitals.com*; *Font:* Primer Print, Internet.

TEN CUTE THINGS HE SAYS *by Leah LaMontagne.* **Supplies** *Cardstock:* Bazzill Basics Paper; *Patterned paper:* Keeping Memories Alive; *Chipboard, round letters, felt flower and brads:* Queen & Co.; *Paint and rub-ons:* Making Memories; *Pen:* Zig Writer, EK Success.

DID YOU NOTICE?

Journaling is a snap when you list memorable sayings. Use brads or other decorative elements in place of bullet points.

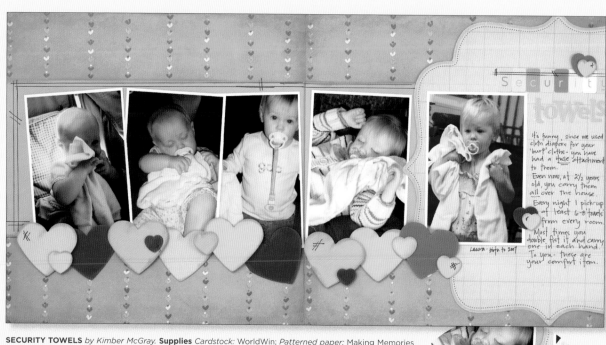

SECURITY TOWELS *by Kimber McGray.* **Supplies** *Cardstock:* WorldWin; *Patterned paper:* Making Memories and We R Memory Keepers; *Letter stickers:* KI Memories and Making Memories; *Ink:* ColorBox, Clearsnap; *Punches:* Creative Memories and Marvy Uchida; *Pens:* American Crafts; Zig Writer, EK Success.

DID YOU NOTICE?

You can create a fun border using shaped punches, such as hearts. Just punch the shape from various colors of cardstock and arrange them as a border under your photos.

FIRST GRADE *by Deena Wuest.* **Supplies** *Software:* Adobe Photoshop Elements 4.0, Adobe Systems; *Digital paper:* MonoBlendz Paperie Aqua by Anna Aspnes, *www.designerdigitals.com*; *Digital edge accents:* Graphic Pop Edgers No. 2 by Katie Pertiet, *www.designerdigitals.com*; *Digital date accent:* Digital Date Stamps Vol. 6 by Katie Pertiet, *www.designerdigitals.com*; *Fonts:* Impact and Minion Pro, Internet.

student council

Miquelle

2007-2008
6th Grade

Miquelle made a goal this year to be on the student council. She has had a great time so far. She has attended an all day leadership training at BYU, helped with the book fair, and helped organize a school service project. She has made new friends and learned a lot.

STUDENT COUNCIL *by Bonnie Lotz.* **Supplies** *Patterned paper:* Creative Imaginations (number) and Scrapbook Wizard (red gingham); *Lettering template:* ScrapPagerz; *Brad:* Making Memories; *Font:* Century Gothic, Microsoft; *Other:* Notebook and cork paper.

sOfTball '07

dad talKed You into PLaYing Softball again this Summer

Your team was called the SCRaPPERS

You had two REaLLY good and fun coaches

You EnjoYEd PLaYing and EVEn hit Your fiRSt homERun

it S obvious YoU RE a VERY taLEntEd Softball PLaYER

WE aRE So PRoud of You!

SOFTBALL *by Wendy Anderson.* **Supplies** *Cardstock:* Bazzill Basics Paper; *Letter stickers:* Making Memories; *Die cut:* Paper House Productions; *Metal accents:* 7gypsies (arrow turn) and American Crafts (photo corner); *Brad:* Doodlebug Design; *Font:* 2Peas Graham Cracker, www.twopeasinabucket.com.

DID YOU NOTICE?

Wendy added a fun touch to her journaling strips by using a different color for each line of journaling.

dad talKed You into PLaYing S

YoUR team was calLEd thE SCR

You had two REaLLY good and f

You EnjoYEd PLaYing and EVE

it S obvious YoU RE a VERY t

E aRE So PRoud of Y

ADULTS

Although kids are often the focus of scrapbook layouts, the story of your life—your history, goals, activities and aspirations—is just as important to future generations. Be sure to complete some "all about me" layouts to ensure *you* are a part of your family albums.

THE NOT SO AFFECTIONATE SISTER by Suzy Plantamura. **Supplies** *Cardstock:* Bazzill Basics Paper; *Patterned paper, chipboard circle, arrow die cut and word stickers:* Scenic Route; *Letter stickers:* American Crafts; *Pens:* EK Success.

HILDEGAARD *by Amber Ries. Photos by Susan Easley.* **Supplies** *Software:* Adobe Photoshop CS2, Adobe Systems; *Digital paper:* Colors Paper Pack and A Day for a Daydream Paper Pack by Jesse Edwards, www.designerdigitals.com; *Digital buttons:* Button Brights by Anna Aspnes, www.designerdigitals.com; *Digital photo corners:* Korner Plumes No. 2 by Anna Aspnes, www.designerdigitals.com; *Digital buttons:* Botanist Notebook No. 04 Kit by Katie Pertiet, www.designerdigitals.com; Plastic Buttons by Katie Pertiet, www.designerdigitals.com; *Digital title:* Polar Escape Kit by Katie Pertiet, www.designerdigitals.com; *Digital stitching and frog closures:* Letter Box Seamstress Kit by Katie Pertiet, www.designerdigitals.com; *Digital drop shadow:* Drop Shadow Action Set by Katie Pertiet, www.designerdigitals.com; *Font:* Times New Roman, Microsoft.

DID YOU NOTICE?

For an eye-catching title, Amber used the "@" symbol in place of one of the "a's."

IF THINGS WERE UP TO ME by Suzy Plantamura. **Supplies** Cardstock: Bazzill Basics Paper; Patterned paper: Best Creation; Letter stickers: American Crafts; Pen: Sakura.

ALL DECKED OUT by Kimber McGray. **Supplies** *Patterned paper:* Jenni Bowlin Studio; *Letter stickers and pen:* American Crafts; *Brads:* Making Memories.

DID YOU NOTICE?

Most of the elements on this two-page layout are contained in the center. Notice how the title and photos are placed so they cross over the page division.

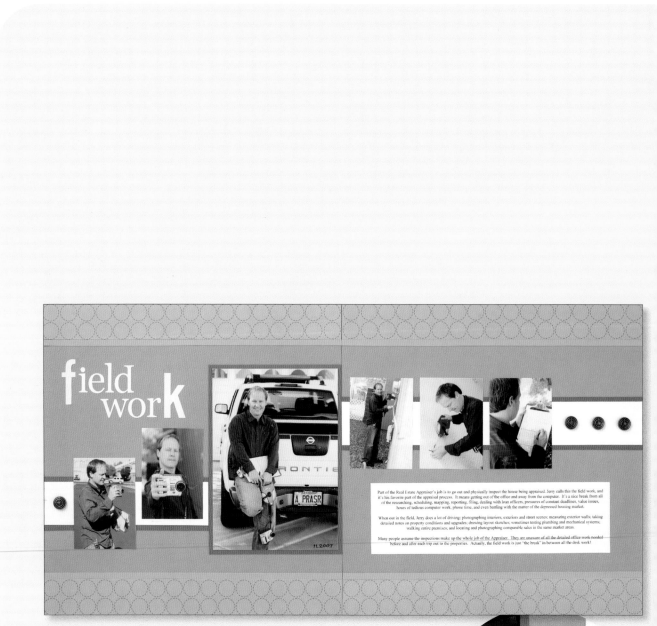

FIELD WORK *by Leah LaMontagne.* **Supplies** *Cardstock:* Bazzill Basics Paper; *Patterned paper:* SEI; *Letter stickers:* Chatterbox and Memories Complete; *Font:* Times New Roman, Microsoft; *Other:* Brads.

DID YOU NOTICE?

Using strips of patterned paper as your page borders, you can create a consistent design across a two-page spread.

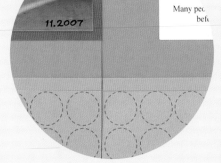

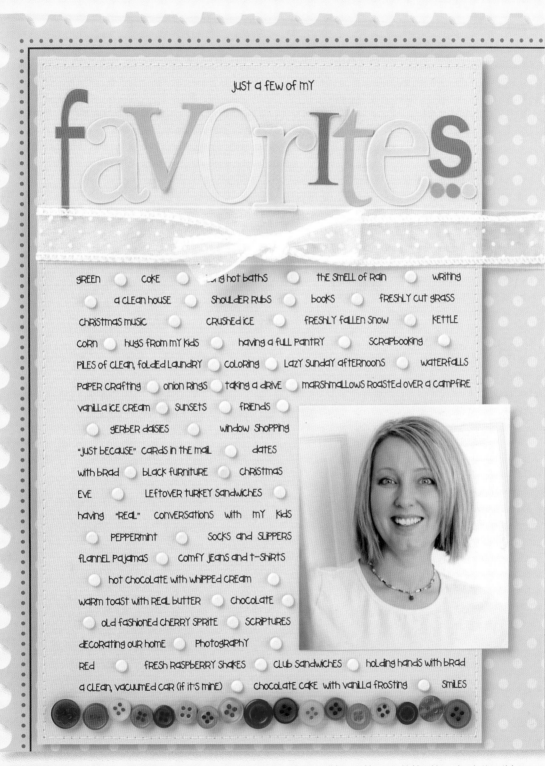

just a few of my

faVOrItes...

green • coke • long hot baths • the smell of rain • writing • a clean house • shoulder rubs • books • freshly cut grass • christmas music • crushed ice • freshly fallen snow • kettle corn • hugs from my kids • having a full pantry • scrapbooking • piles of clean, folded laundry • coloring • lazy sunday afternoons • waterfalls • paper crafting • onion rings • taking a drive • marshmallows roasted over a campfire • vanilla ice cream • sunsets • friends • gerber daisies • window shopping • "just because" cards in the mail • dates with brad • black furniture • christmas eve • leftover turkey sandwiches • having "real" conversations with my kids • peppermint • socks and slippers • flannel pajamas • comfy jeans and t-shirts • hot chocolate with whipped cream • warm toast with real butter • chocolate • old fashioned cherry sprite • scriptures • decorating our home • photography • red • fresh raspberry shakes • club sandwiches • holding hands with brad • a clean, vacuumed car (if it's mine) • chocolate cake with vanilla frosting • smiles

FAVORITES by Wendy Anderson. **Supplies** Cardstock: Chatterbox; Patterned paper, ribbon and buttons: Making Memories; Letter stickers: Making Memories (teal) and Three Bugs in a Rug (pink and green); Brads: Doodlebug Design; Font: 2Peas Graham Cracker, www.two-peasinabucket.com; Other: Thread.

FAMILY AND FRIENDS

Laughs, tears. Inside jokes, arguments. Bonding, sharing, supporting. The moments we share with family and friends enrich our lives. Design layouts that capture what you've done with them, what you've learned from them, what you look back on . . . and look forward to.

BEST FRIENDS *by Suzy Plantamura.* **Supplies** *Patterned paper:* Autumn Leaves (green), Paper Salon (yellow) and Sassafras Lass (red); *Letter stickers:* American Crafts; *Rub-ons:* Die Cuts With a View; *Felt flower:* Prima; *Embroidery floss:* DMC; *Pen:* Sakura; *Other:* Button.

14 things I admire about

mY {litTLe} BroTHer.

1 he is ALWAYS willing to help me with my computer issues - no matter how late it is

2 he is funny and has a great sense of humor

3 he has always been good at putting things together

4 he is an awesome dad to Dax

5 he is one of the most non-judgmental people I know

6 he is like a big kid

7 he is a self-taught computer genius

8 he has a great smile and gorgeous eyes

9 he doesn't care when my house is mess

10 he makes yummy fruit salad

11 he is patient with Daxen and his nieces and nephews

12 he is modest and has no idea how much potential he has

13 he is generous and shares movies and games all the time

14 he will be an incredible husband to someone someday

MY LITTLE BROTHER by Wendy Anderson. **Supplies** *Patterned paper:* American Crafts and KI Memories; *Letter stickers:* KI Memories and ScrapPagerz; *Chipboard brackets:* American Crafts; *Paint:* Making Memories; *Font:* Microsoft Sans Serif, Microsoft.

DAD *by Bonnie Lotz.* **Supplies** *Patterned paper and chipboard letters:* Collage Press; *Letter stamps:* PSX Design; *Brads and button:* Making Memories; *Font:* CK Constitution, *www.scrapnfonts.com.*

DID YOU NOTICE?

You can include journaling from each family member on your layout. Here, Bonnie included some personal notes from each child beneath the photos.

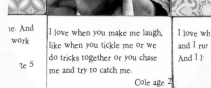

FRIENDS, FOOD, FUN *by Kimber McGray.* **Supplies** *Cardstock:* WorldWin; *Patterned paper:* Bo-Bunny Press and Scenic Route; *Letter stickers:* Arctic Frog, Chatterbox and KI Memories; *Pen:* American Crafts.

DID YOU NOTICE?

Kimber used a different style of letter sticker for each line of her title.

Experiment with different styles for fun title treatments.

What Were THEY Thinking

?

No, I didn't become a smoker; I don't watch THAT much T.V, and I didn't become a serial killer. It was the 1970's and I really did have great parents, but I do have to wonder about some of their photo choices. (I left out the numerous photos of me running around naked.)

I sure was a cute thing though.

WHAT WERE THEY THINKING? *by Carey Johnson.* **Supplies** *Patterned paper:* Autumn Leaves; *Chipboard accents:* Heidi Swapp for Advantus; *Brad:* Making Memories; *Font:* Arial Black, Microsoft.

make lots of messes * have a bath (be sure to do plenty of splashing) * eat some cereal * play the spin around and fall down game * play outside (stop to look at a bug) * stop for a snack* make more messes * time for lunch * have a NAP* run as fast as you can* read some books* time for more messes * watch sesame street * eat dinner * help with the dishes (play in the bubbles) * read more books * brush teeth * hugs and kisses for all Just another ordinary day for Cole and Cagney

Let's play

2 {two}

A day in the life of two busy two year olds

A DAY IN THE LIFE by Bonnie Lotz. **Supplies** *Patterned paper and ribbon:* SEI; *Letter stickers:* Sonburn; *Rub-ons:* Doodlebug Design; *Font:* CK Handprint, www.scrapnfonts.com.

DID YOU NOTICE?

Punctuation marks are useful for adding emphasis to titles; Bonnie used brackets to create a space for hers.

HERITAGE

The first scrapbook you ever saw may have been a heritage album with a collection of photos of ancestors from your family tree. Keep up the tradition with pages that showcase days gone by and compare past to present. Offer details about your great-grandparents, grandparents, parents and even you as a child.

9 MONTHS *by Kimber McGray.* **Supplies** *Patterned paper and stickers:* Making Memories; *Envelope:* WorldWin; *Pens:* American Crafts; Uni-ball Signo, Sanford.

The big sister

Three little sisters, all born one year after the other. Close in age, and close in heart. My Mom, Julie, was the big sister...the ring leader...the "boss". They shared a room together, and just about everything else. Playing with dolls and playing in the backyard were their favorite things to do together as little girls (not to mention be little mothers to their baby brother!). Here they are, in their Easter dresses and scarves from Germany. All lined up in a row from oldest to youngest: Julie, Debbie, Laurie. Throughout the years these three were often found side by side, enjoying life together...always looked after by the big sister. Circa 1963, probably 4, 3, and 2 years old.

THE BIG SISTER by Leah LaMontagne. **Supplies** *Patterned paper:* American Crafts; *Paint:* Making Memories; *Chipboard accent, flowers and brads:* Queen & Co.; *Font:* Chaucer, Internet.

DID YOU NOTICE?

Leah created the stems for this darling flower accent with strips of cardstock. Consider ways to use your paper scraps to create unique page accents.

Unfortunately, I don't remember my Great-Grandfather Frank very well, so I always think of their house as "Grandma Tina's" house (although I found out later in life she didn't care for 'Tina'...she preferred Christina.

Things I remember about visiting my Great Grandma Christina's home:

1. Lawrence Welk on the T.V.
2. Showing off my somersaults in the living room.
3. Many roses in the garden
4. Many flowers on the wallpaper.
5. Grandma Tina always had her hair & makeup done.
6. The smell of food cooking in the kitchen.

TINA by Carey Johnson. **Supplies** *Patterned paper and chipboard letters:* Cosmo Cricket; *Flower:* Bazzill Basics Paper; *Brad:* Stemma; *Font:* Arial Black, Microsoft; *Other:* Antique homemade tatting.

DID YOU NOTICE?

Carey added a soft touch to her layout with delicate accents, such as a crochet flower and a lace border.

In order to play high school football, my grandfather had to rise early in the morning to chore by himself while his other brothers who didn't go to school, slept late. He also had to agree to do chores after football practice, keep up his grades and walk to school. Despite breaking his collar bone, he loved playing football. Out of his family of 17, Arnold was the only one to graduate high school. This is just one of the many examples of his hard work ethic and dedication.

FOOTBALL *by Deena Wuest.* **Supplies** *Software:* Adobe Photoshop Elements 4.0, Adobe Systems; *Digital accent:* Sweet Mystery Kit by Jennifer Adams Donnelly, *www.designerdigitals.com*; *Digital paper:* Sacked Harvest Paper Pack by Katie Pertiet, *www.designerdigitals.com*; *Digital date accent:* Digital Date Stamps Vol. 3 by Katie Pertiet, *www.designerdigitals.com*; *Digital frame:* Vintage Photo Frames by Katie Pertiet, *www.designerdigitals.com*; *Digital overlay:* Grunge Overlays by Katie Pertiet, *www.designerdigitals.com*; *Fonts:* Book Antigua and Dichotomy, Internet.

BROTHERS & SISTERS *by Bonnie Lotz.* **Supplies** *Patterned paper:* Die Cuts With a View; *Letter stickers:* Creative Imaginations; *Stickers:* KI Memories; *Font:* CK Constitution, *www.scrapnfonts.com.*

The Hartmanns
Rochester, MN
Silver Lake Park

Yeah, it is hard to believe, but my parents did have a life B.C (before Carey). They were a young couple. My mom worked for an interior decorator and my dad was working at Methodist Hospital...and they were oh-so-hip and stylish in their 1970 duds.

THE HARTMANNS *by Carey Johnson.* **Supplies** *Software:* Adobe Photoshop CS2, Adobe Systems; *Patterned paper:* My Mind's Eye; *Chipboard letters:* Pressed Petals; *Circle accent:* Technique Tuesday; *Digital brush:* Little Grove Brushes & Rub-Ons by Tia Bennett, *www.two-peasinabucket.com*; *Fonts:* Arial Black and Century Gothic, Microsoft.

HOLIDAYS

Holidays are not only days that celebrate events, but also occasions to gather with family, bask in tradition and eat a lot of delicious food. What do you look forward to each year? Create pages about those parties, decorations, games, meals, gifts, festivals and surprises.

VALENTINE'S DAY by *Wendy Anderson*. **Supplies** *Cardstock:* Bazzill Basics Paper; *Patterned paper:* Scenic Route; *Stickers:* Doodlebug Design and Scenic Route; *Rub-ons:* Heidi Grace for Fiskars (birds) and Making Memories (text); *Ribbon:* Bo-Bunny Press; *Tag rim and eyelet:* Making Memories; *Gems:* Heidi Swapp for Advantus; *Photo corners:* American Crafts; *Font:* Rebekah's Birthday, Internet; *Other:* Thread.

seek

more than the egg

The egg. There it is. Just waiting for you to discover it. To claim it. To enjoy it. It's the same with God's word. It's waiting just for you. I pray you will always seek it out. EASTER 2006

SEEK by Deena Wuest. **Supplies** Software: Adobe Photoshop Elements 4.0, Adobe Systems; Digital paper: MonoBlendz Paperie Aqua by Anna Aspnes, www.designerdigitals.com; Digital frame: Frame It II Custom Shapes by Anna Aspnes, www.designerdigitals.com; Digital brush-strokes: Brushstrokes by Kellie Mize, www.designerdigitals.com; Fonts: Avant Garde and Impact, Internet.

HOORAY FOR THE USA *by Leah LaMontagne.* **Supplies** *Cardstock:* Bazzill Basics Paper; *Letter stickers:* Chatterbox and Making Memories (glittered); *Date stamp:* Technique Tuesday; *Ink:* Stampin' Up!; *Brads:* Queen & Co.; *Label:* Paper Reflections.

DID YOU NOTICE?

Featuring six vertical 4" x 6" prints along the bottom of a 12" x 12" spread is a great way to showcase several photos from a single event.

THE JOYS OF HALLOWEEN *by Deena Wuest.* **Supplies** *Software:* Adobe Photoshop Elements 4.0, Adobe Systems; *Digital paper:* MonoBlendz Paperie Cayenne by Anna Aspnes, *www.designerdigitals.com*; *Digital overlay:* Happy Halloween Page Set by Anna Aspnes, *www.designerdigitals.com*; *Digital paper (black):* Purely Happy Paper by Katie Pertiet, *www.designerdigitals.com*; *Digital frame:* Hinged Photo Frames by Katie Pertiet, *www.designerdigitals.com*; *Digital date accent:* Digital Date Stamps Vol. 6 by Katie Pertiet, *www.designerdigitals.com*; *Fonts:* Avant Garde and Establo, Internet.

THANKSGIVING *by Bonnie Lotz.* **Supplies** *Patterned paper:* Daisy D's Paper Co. (yellow), Rusty Pickle (red) and Scrapbook Wizard (green); *Leaf transparency:* Creative Imaginations; *Letter stamps:* Ma Vinci's Reliquary; *Rub-ons:* Doodlebug Design; *Brads and photo anchors:* Making Memories; *Ribbon:* May Arts; *Font:* CK Stenography, *www.scrapnfonts.com.*

DID YOU NOTICE?

Journaling can be as simple as adding short captions to photos. Here, Bonnie used paper scraps to add notes about each photo.

CHRISTMAS TREE by Amber Ries. **Supplies** *Software:* Adobe Photoshop CS2, Adobe Systems; *Digital paper:* Polar Escape Paper Pack by Katie Pertiet and Curled Notebook Paper by Katie Pertiet, *www.designerdigitals.com*; *Digital overlay:* Grungy Overlays by Katie Pertiet, *www.designerdigitals.com*; *Digital epoxy accents:* Joyful Epoxies by Katie Pertiet, *www.designerdigitals.com*; *Digital jewelry tag:* Blueline Botanicals Kit by Katie Pertiet, *www.designerdigitals.com*; *Digital word accents:* Holiday Dots by Katie Pertiet, *www.designerdigitals.com*; *Digital Christmas tree:* Holiday Trees No. 3 Brushes-n-Stamps by Katie Pertiet, *www.designerdigitals.com*; *Digital frame:* Storyboard Frames No. 1 (altered) and Curled Photo Frames (altered) by Katie Pertiet, *www.designerdigitals.com*; *Digital ribbon:* Frayed Knots by Lynn Grieveson, *www.designerdigitals.com*; *Digital trees and snowflakes:* Polar Escape by Pattie Knox, *www.designerdigitals.com*; *Digital letters:* Glitzy Chips Alphabet by Pattie Knox, *www.designerdigitals.com*; *Digital paper:* Little Creepers Page Kit (purple) by Mindy Terasawa, *www.designerdigitals.com*; *Digital paper:* Jubilant (dark brown) by Gina Cabrera, *www.designerdigitals.com*; *Digital title block:* Falling for You, *www.designerdigitals.com*; *Digital paper:* Smarshmallows (white), *www.theshabbyshoppe.com*; *Digital paper:* A Merry Little Christmas (green) by Michelle Coleman, *www.littledreamerdesigns.com*; *Digital paper:* Share in the Season (red) by Sara Carling, *www.scrapbookgraphics.com*; *Fonts:* More Than Enough, Sharon Classic and Splendid 66, Internet.

CELEBRATIONS

Sandwiched between traditional holidays are the other celebrations in our lives honoring achievements, relationships, community or simply turning a year older. Commemorate these moments—big and small—with a layout detailing the who, what, where, when and why.

Nine years of marriage
A wonderful family
loving you more with each
passing year! 05-07

YEAR 9 *by Suzy Plantamura.* **Supplies** *Patterned paper:* KI Memories and Scenic Route; *Lace paper:* KI Memories; *Rub-on letters:* me & my BIG ideas; *Paint:* Delta Creative; *Hearts:* Heidi Swapp for Advantus; *Pens:* Sakura.

Our

L I M O

awaits

...and await it did! Our wedding party photos took a very long time, but our ride stood by. Jerry arranged for a classic white limousine to escort us to our reception. We chose to make the trip all alone, just the two of us. We enjoyed a few minutes to relax and actually take in what had just happened...we got hitched, we did it! We're finally married! Now on to the party!!!

Jerry & Leah

OUR LIMO AWAITS *by Leah LaMontagne.* **Supplies** *Software:* Adobe Photoshop 7.0, Adobe Systems; *Patterned paper:* Déjà Views by The C-Thru Ruler Co. and KI Memories; *Letter and circle stickers:* Déjà Views by The C-Thru Ruler Co.; *Stamps:* Technique Tuesday; *Ink:* Stampin' Up!; *Brads:* Making Memories (decorative) and Queen & Co. (mini); *Digital label:* Swank Labels by Jennifer Pebbles, *www.twopeasinabucket.com*; *Fonts:* Edwardian Script and Vetren, Internet.

PARK *by Bonnie Lotz.* **Supplies** *Patterned paper:* Bo-Bunny Press; *Letter and number stamps:* PSX Design; *Tags:* Bo-Bunny Press (text) and Making Memories (chipboard); *Ribbon:* Scrapbook Wizard; *Font:* CK Newsprint, *www.scrapnfonts.com.*

DID YOU NOTICE?

Bonnie's layout design is based on a grid. The title and journaling block are the same size and are framed by photos of all their activities.

A VERY MELMO BIRTHDAY *by Amber Ries.* **Supplies** *Software:* Adobe Photoshop CS2, Adobe Systems; *Digital paper:* Botanist Notebook No. 9 Kit (dark brown), Krafty Ledger Paper Pack, Spot Dots Paper Pack (orange) and Perfect Pets Paper Pack (stripe) by Katie Pertiet, *www.designerdigitals.com*; *Digital frame:* Postage Stamp Frames No. 2 by Katie Pertiet, *www.designerdigitals.com*; *Digital postage stamp:* Postmark Celebrations Brushes-n-Stamps by Katie Pertiet, *www.designerdigitals.com*; *Digital letter cards:* Krafty Bits Alphabet by Katie Pertiet, *www.designerdigitals.com*; *Digital stitched strips:* Stitched Chip Strips by Katie Pertiet, *www.designerdigitals.com*; *Digital drop shadow:* Drop Shadow Action Set by Katie Pertiet, *www.designerdigitals.com*; *Digital felt letters:* True Love Felt Alphabet by Pattie Knox, *www.designerdigitals.com*; *Digital felt balloon:* Hoppy Birthday Page Kit by Pattie Knox, *www.designerdigitals.com*; *Digital twill labels:* Birthday Boy Kit by Dana Zarling, *www.designerdigitals.com*; *Digital gift accents:* Tracy Robinson, *www.tracyanndigitalart.com*; *Digital paper:* Smarshmallows (white), *www.theshabbyshoppe.com*; *Font:* Times New Roman, Microsoft.

Seven years and we have yet to take a single family vacation. Instead, we have established a family tradition. Every birthday we load up and spend an evening at the indoor water park followed by pizza from Ken's. Every birthday. Whether rain or shine (or snow). It's a great reminder of how lucky we are to be a family. It's a great way to re-connect. It's become our favorite

family **TRADITION**

Savanna's 7th birthday

FAMILY TRADITION *by Deena Wuest.* **Supplies** *Software:* Adobe Photoshop Elements 4.0, Adobe Systems; *Digital paper:* Surfer Dude Paper Pack by Katie Pertiet, *www.designerdigitals.com*; *Digital frame:* Dried Brush Frames Brushes-n-Stamps by Katie Pertiet, *www.designerdigitals.com*; *Digital overlay:* Watery Overlays by Katie Pertiet, *www.designerdigitals.com*; *Fonts:* Avant Garde and Eight Track, Internet.

Retirement

bliss

They were married in 1956

6 kids, 10 houses,

10 cities, and 8 jobs later

they have reached retirement.

Enjoy it, you deserve it!

RETIREMENT BLISS *by Bonnie Lotz.* **Supplies** *Patterned paper:* Bo-Bunny Press; *Heart accent:* Hand-cut from cardstock; *Letter stamps:* Stampendous!; *Word tag:* Making Memories; *Rickrack:* May Arts; *Font:* CK Constitution, *www.scrapnfonts.com.*

VACATIONS

Whether your last excursion was relaxing, awe-inspiring, adventure-packed or educational, scrapbook the photos and memories so you can relive them again and again. Remember, a "vacation" can be a trip to Paris or a trip to the zoo. It doesn't matter how far you were from home . . . as long as you enjoyed yourself!

CASEY JONES *by Amber Ries. Photos by Susan Easley.* **Supplies** *Software:* Adobe Photoshop CS2, Adobe Systems; *Digital paper:* Big Boy Page Kit (white) by Dana Zarling, *www.designerdigitals.com; Digital photo anchors:* MetalMix Element Set No. 01 by Anna Aspnes, *www.designerdigitals.com; Digital paper:* Along for the Ride Kit (curved paper) by Lynn Grieveson, *www.designerdigitals.com; Digital ribbon:* Frayed Knots by Lynn Grieveson, *www.designerdigitals.com; Digital felt letters:* Katie's Jewel's Felt Alphabet Collection by Pattie Knox, *www.designerdigitals.com; Digital felt train:* Hoppy Birthday Page Kit by Pattie Knox, *www.designerdigitals.com; Digital negative frame:* Storyboard Negatives by Katie Pertiet, *www.designerdigitals.com; Digital tag:* Mega Tag Pack by Katie Pertiet; *Digital drop shadow:* Drop Shadow Action Set by Katie Pertiet, *www.designerdigitals.com; Digital papers:* Tracy Robinson, *www.tracyanndigitalart.com; Font:* Pooh, Internet.

LEGOLAND RIDES *by Leah LaMontagne.* **Supplies** *Patterned paper:* BasicGrey and Scenic Route; *Chipboard letters:* Provo Craft; *Letter stamps:* Hero Arts; *Ink:* Stampin' Up!; *Brads:* Queen & Co.; *Ribbon:* SEI; *Pens:* Uni-ball Signo, Sanford; Zig Writer, EK Success.

DID YOU NOTICE?
Tags are perfect for adding small journaling blocks!

HUGE PRIDE *by Kimber McGray.* **Supplies** *Cardstock:* WorldWin; *Patterned paper:* Sassafras Lass; *Letter stickers:* Chatterbox and Making Memories; *Stickers:* Scenic Route; *Clip:* Making Memories; *Pen:* American Crafts.

DID YOU NOTICE?

Lined paper is great for handwritten journaling, whether you write on the lines directly or use them as a guide, as Kimber's done here.

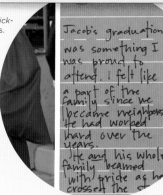

EXPLORING SAINT KITTS by *Suzy Plantamura.* **Supplies** *Cardstock:* Bazzill Basics Paper and WorldWin; *Patterned paper:* Creative Imaginations and KI Memories; *Letter stickers:* K&Company; *Pens:* Zig Writer, EK Success; *Other:* Heart sticker.

5 DAYS *by Wendy Anderson.* **Supplies** *Patterned paper, epoxy buttons, shapes and tag:* Making Memories; *Letter stickers:* Doodlebug Design and ScrapPagerz; *Ribbon:* Creative Impressions (gingham) and Making Memories (orange); *Font:* Pea Yar Yar, Internet; *Other:* Thread.

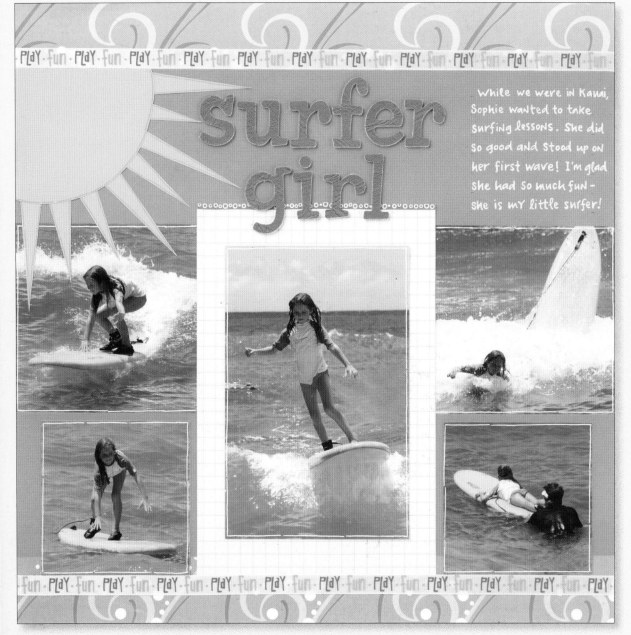

While we were in Kauai, Sophie wanted to take surfing lessons. She did so good and stood up on her first wave! I'm glad she had so much fun - she is my little surfer!

SURFER GIRL *by Suzy Plantamura.* **Supplies** *Patterned paper:* Creative Imaginations and Love, Elsie for KI Memories; *Letter stickers:* American Crafts; *Ribbon:* Love, Elsie for KI Memories; *Pen:* Sakura.

scrapbooking terms

ACCENT
Pre-printed or custom-designed adornment used to decorate a layout. Items can include tags, stickers, rub-ons, buttons, tags, gems and flowers. Also referred to as an "embellishment."

ACID FREE
Acid-free materials are recommended for use on layouts to help preserve photos. Products designated "acid free" have a pH factor of 7 or greater.

ACID MIGRATION
Process in which the harmful acidity of one item affects another.

ACRYLIC PAINT
Water-based, synthetic colorant designed to dry quickly. Medium can be used to alter accents, add color wash, stamp or texturize.

ADHESIVES
Used to adhere photos and embellishments. Available in permanent and repositionable varieties and different forms, such as liquids, dots, tapes, sticks, tabs and sprays.

AGING
Altering cardstock, paper or embellishments to create an antique or distressed finish.

ALBUM
Book that collects and holds layouts with metal rings, coils, hinges or posts. Like all page materials, an album should be archival.

ALTER
To change the appearance of an item, such as patterned paper, accents, composition books or compact discs, with collage, inks, paints, paper or mediums.

ANALOGOUS COLORS
Colors located directly next to one another on a color wheel.

APERTURE
The opening in a camera that opens and closes when the shutter is released to let in light.

ARCHIVAL
Word used to describe products and materials tested and proven to have a safe amount of acidic and buffered content.

AWL
Small, hand-held tool with a tapered, pointed tip used to punch holes in leather and other materials.

BLENDER PEN/PENCIL
A marker or pencil that blends or softens colored pencils, markers, chalks or watercolors.

BONE FOLDER
Curved tool used to impress a crisp crease in a piece of paper or cardstock.

BORDER
Design along the side or periphery of a layout.

BRAD
Metal fastener featuring two prongs that spread in back, butterfly style, to attach items to the background page.

BRASS TEMPLATE
Small, thin piece of brass with shaped cutouts used for dry embossing or stenciling.

BRAYER
Hand-held tool featuring a rubber roller used to spread ink, burnish materials or generate artistic, textured effects.

BUFFERED
With a pH rating of 8.5, paper considered "buffered" features an agent designed to neutralize acidic contaminants.

BURNISH
To press or rub materials firmly with a brayer or bone folder to smooth and adhere.

CARDSTOCK
Richly colored, heavyweight paper ideal for use as page backgrounds and photo mats.

CHALK
Lightweight, powdery medium offered in a range of colors. Applied with a sponge applicator, cotton ball, brush or fingertip.

CHALK INK
A pigment ink that dries to a powdery, muted finish.

CHIPBOARD
Sturdy paperboard often cut into shapes, mini-album pages or frames.

CLIP ART
Available in books, software or online sources, this ready-made artwork can be used as accents or paper-piecing patterns.

COLLAGE
A combination of materials—such as memorabilia, photos, clip art, fabric and paper—brought together for artistic effect. May be sealed with decoupage medium or clear glaze.

COLOR-BLOCKING
Arranging and combining squares of complementary or contrasting colors of cardstock to produce a geometric background.

COLOR WASH
A subtle tint of color generated with a thin layer of water-colors, dye or acrylic paint that's been thinned with water.

COLOR WHEEL
A circular spectrum of colors that shows their relationships. Helpful when selecting or coordinating shades.

COMPLEMENTARY COLORS
Colors situated directly across from one another on a color wheel.

CONCHO
Decorative metal fastener with sharp prongs. Often pushed through cardstock or the center of another accent. Prongs are then pressed flat to secure. Also known as a "nailhead."

CORNER ROUNDER
Hand-held punch that removes the sharp corners from photos, leaving curved edges.

CORRUGATED CARDSTOCK
Cardstock with a wavy, textured surface.

CRIMPER
Hand-held, manually-operated tool featuring two textured rollers. When paper, metal or other malleable materials are run through the crimper, they take on the roller's design or texture.

CROP
To trim a photo. A party or workshop where several scrap-bookers get together to work on layouts is also known as a "crop."

CROPPING
Eliminating unnecessary background or making a photo more appealing by trimming it. The craft of scrapbooking is also known as "cropping."

DEACIDIFICATION SPRAY
Product designed to remove or neutralize acid in paper products and memorabilia like newspaper and certificates.

DEBOSSING
Effect created using the same technique as dry embossing. Instead of showing the image with the raised side up, debossing allows the recessed image to show.

DECORATIVE-EDGE SCISSORS
Scissors featuring a decorative pattern to the blade that produce a fancy edge instead of a straight one.

DECOUPAGE
Creating a collage by layering memorabilia, photos or illustrations, then sealing with a clear glaze or decoupage medium.

DEGRADATION
The breaking down of materials over time, such as paper or photos fading or becoming brown and brittle.

DIE CUT
A shape created with a press and metal-edged "die" that cuts through cardstock or other materials.

DIMENSIONAL ADHESIVE
Type of liquid glue that retains its raised surface after it has dried.

DOUBLE MOUNTED
Photos that are placed on two mats of different sizes, shapes or colors.

DOUBLE-SIDED TAPE
Tape with adhesive on both sides. Thin and lightweight, but strong enough to bond heavy items. Also referred to as "double-stick" tape.

DRY BRUSHING
Applying paint using a stiff-bristled dry brush.

DYE INK
Water-based stamping ink that dries quickly. Check to be sure the pad is labeled "permanent" and "acid free."

EMBELLISHMENT

An accent, decoration or adornment used to dress up a layout. Buttons, chipboard shapes, die cuts and ribbon are all considered "embellishments."

EMBOSS

Generating an image with a raised surface either with pressure (dry embossing) or with a special powder and heat gun (heat embossing).

EMBOSSING GUN

Tool designed to melt embossing powder with heat. Also known as a "heat gun."

EMBOSSING INK

Glycerin-based clear or slightly tinted sticky ink designed for use with rubber stamps and embossing powder.

EMBOSSING PEN

Embossing ink contained in a handy pen. Used to create embossed lettering or to apply ink to small areas.

EMBOSSING POWDER

Clear or colored powder applied over wet ink and heated to produce a shiny, raised image.

ENCAPSULATION

Sealing memorabilia or dimensional items in archival plastic to prevent the item's acid from migrating and damaging nearby photos.

EPHEMERA

Nostalgic items like letters, postcards and vintage pieces used in decoupage or collage. Sometimes used as another term for memorabilia.

EYELET

A fastener, typically with a hole in the center, that's inserted through a punched hole and flattened with the tap of a hammer. Also known as a "grommet."

EYELET SETTER

Hand-held, metal tool with a cone- or star shaped tip. When used in conjunction with a hammer, the setter flattens the back of a snap or eyelet. New spring-loaded versions can set eyelets without a hammer.

FIBER

String-like embellishment offered in a variety of colors and thicknesses. Often used as accents to top tags, hang charms or tie other embellishments together.

FILM SPEED

Term that describes a film's sensitivity to light, indicated by its "ISO" (a standard from the International Organization for Standardization). On digital cameras, the user can choose the camera's ISO.

FIXATIVE

Spray designed to seal and protect artwork from smearing. Dries to a matte or glossy finish.

FOCAL POINT

An element in a photograph or on a layout specifically designed or positioned to catch the viewer's eye.

FONT

A style of lettering. Rubber stamps, stickers, rub-ons and type styles on the computer are all offered in different fonts.

GEL MEDIUM

Gel designed to create texture, blend with other mediums or transfer images.

GEL PEN

Type of pen featuring smooth-flowing, opaque, metallic or colored ink. Some varieties are suitable for writing and doodling on dark paper.

GENEALOGY

The research of a person's line of ancestry.

GESSO

Water-based paint (sometimes a mixture of whiting and glue) used to prepare a surface for painting or gilding.

GLUE STICK

Paste-type adhesive contained in a swivel-up tube. Good for affixing photos and lightweight elements. Be sure to check for the terms "photo safe" or "acid free."

GOLD-LEAF FLAKE

Feather-light, metallic flakes applied to a surface with adhesive, glaze or double-stick tape to create a textured, shiny finish.

GREASE PENCILS

Soft pencils (typically in orange or black) designed to be used on photos. Also known as "wax pencils."

GROMMET

A fastener, typically with a hole in the center, that's inserted through a punched hole and flattened with the tap of a hammer. Also known as an "eyelet."

GUM ARABIC

A water-soluble medium used as a binder for pigment powders or to add depth to prints.

HALF-PINT
Mini album that is half the size of a traditional book. Typically a three-ring binder that holds 8½″ x 5½″ layouts.

HEAT GUN
Tool designed to melt embossing powder with heat. Also known as an "embossing gun."

HERITAGE LAYOUTS
Pages featuring heritage photos or the stories of your ancestors.

HERITAGE PHOTOS
Vintage prints of your family, ancestors, community, personal or world history.

HOT-FOIL PEN
Hand-held, battery-operated tool used in conjunction with special foil paper. The pen's plastic tip heats up to transfer foil to paper, generating metallic designs.

HOT GLUE
Adhesive, originally in stick form, melted via an electric "gun" and used to bond a variety of materials.

IDEA BOOK
A book or special magazine issue featuring techniques, tips or layouts designed to teach or inspire crafters.

INTERMEDIATE COLORS
Blends of primary and secondary colors, like red-orange. Also known as "tertiary colors."

ISO
Rating that indicates a film's sensitivity to light. Derived from a standard from the International Organization for Standardization. A photographer is able to manually choose the camera's ISO on digital cameras.

JEWELER'S TAGS
Tags used by jewelers to add prices to rings and other jewelry. Used by scrapbookers as accents to add dates or other short messages to cards or layouts.

JEWELRY FINDINGS
Components used to make jewelry that are also used as page accents. Can include hooks, clips, filigree pieces or chains.

JOURNALING
Adding text to a layout to provide details, dates or the story and emotions behind the photos. The actual text on the page is also referred to as "journaling."

JUTE
String-like accent manufactured from plant fibers.

LAMINATION
Sealing an item between translucent material in an attempt to preserve or protect it.

LAYER
To create dimension, texture or interest by overlapping cardstock, photos, accents or other materials.

LAYOUT
Page designed to showcase photos, memorabilia and written memories.

LETTERING TEMPLATES
Thin plastic pieces with the alphabet cut out, designed to be traced to create letter shapes.

LIGHT BOX
Small electric or battery-operated light source used to view shapes while dry embossing.

LIGHTFAST
Way to describe material that's resistant and colorfast to sunlight.

LIGNIN
An acidic substance, sometimes used to bond wood fibers, that breaks down over time. Paper that is not lignin-free is likely to become brittle and yellow as it ages.

LSS
Slang abbreviation for "local scrapbook store."

MAGNETIC ALBUM
Photo album featuring adhesive-coated pages designed to hold images in place. Photos should be removed from any existing magnetic albums as soon as possible since they are not archival.

MASK
Plastic pieces, often backed with temporary adhesive and pre-cut into a decorative shape. Mask is affixed to the background, then washed over with paint, chalk or other mediums. When the mask is removed, the original background shows through the design.

MASKING
Covering portions of a stamped design to preserve them while surrounding sections are being colored.

MATTING
Adhering a photo by placing it on a piece of cardstock or patterned paper before affixing it to the background.

MEMORABILIA
Pieces that commemorate events, vacations or special moments. Items may include certificates, newspaper clippings, brochures, receipts or ticket stubs.

MESH
Net-like material used to add texture and depth to projects. Offered in paper, metal and plastic.

METALLIC RUB-ONS
Creamy medium that adds metallic highlights and sheen. Applied with fingertips, sponges or brushes.

MINI BOOK
Album much smaller than the traditional 12" x 12" or 8½" x 11". Offered in premade packages or custom created with ribbon, rings or brads as bindings.

MIXED MEDIA
Term used to describe combining two or more types of artistic media, like painting and collage, in a single piece of artwork.

MONOCHROMATIC
Color scheme featuring different shades of a single color.

MOSAIC
Design created with a multitude of smaller pieces. For example, cardstock can be torn or cut into tiny shards and reassembled with white space in between to look like a traditional mosaic.

MOUNT
To affix a photograph, accent or journaling block.

MULBERRY PAPER
Fibrous specialty paper that can be torn or stamped. Produces a feathery edge when torn.

MUTED COLORS
Subtle, as opposed to vibrant, shades of a color.

NAILHEAD
Decorative metal fastener with sharp prongs. Often pushed through cardstock or the center of another accent. Prongs are then pressed flat to secure. Also known as a "concho."

NEGATIVE PIECE
The "outline" that's left on the backing of a sticker or chipboard sheet once the actual shape has been used. Can be cut apart and used on the page or as a "stencil" to create additional looks.

PH LEVEL
A number that reflects the acidity or alkalinity of paper.

PAGE PROTECTORS
Archival pocket sheets designed to hold and display layouts within an album.

PAPER PIECING
Trimming and layering pieces of cardstock, patterned paper or fabric to create a multi-colored design.

PAPER PIERCER
Hand-held, metal tool with a needle-like point used to poke small holes in cardstock.

PAPER PIERCING
Form of paper crafting in which a piercer is used to punch holes in vellum-like paper to produce an elaborate, textured design.

PAPER TRIMMER
Manual tool that trims and cuts cardstock, photos and other materials. Offered in diverse sizes from portable to tabletop and with different types of blades (rotary, decorative, personal safety blades and guillotine arms).

PATTERNED PAPER
Decorative paper completely covered with a textured tint, pattern or design.

PHOTO ACTIVITY TEST
Also known as "P.A.T." Test by the American National Standards Institute that reveals if a product is safe to use with photos.

PHOTO CORNERS
Small, adhesive-backed triangles designed to adhere to the page and secure a photo without applying adhesive to the photo itself.

PHOTO SAFE
Items and materials tested and proven to be acid and lignin free and therefore safe to use on or around photos.

PHOTO TAB
Double-sided adhesive tab. Tabs are typically square shaped with a thin paper backing that must be removed manually.

PHOTO TURN
Small metal embellishment, often adhered with a mini brad and designed to hold a photo in place.

PICK-UP SQUARE
Hard rubber square (resembling an eraser) used to remove excess adhesive.

PIGMENT INK
Opaque, fade-resistant and permanent type of stamping ink. Slow-drying and ideal for heat embossing.

PIGMENT POWDER
Lightweight powder in rich colors, often extracted from different minerals. Can be combined with gum arabic, paint, inks and other mediums to generate textured finishes.

POCKET
Embellishment designed to hold memorabilia, journaling or additional photos on a layout. Pockets can be created with cardstock or photos. Envelopes, library pockets and credit card envelopes can also be used as pockets.

POLYVINYL CHLORIDE
Also known as "PVC," it's a substance shown to be harmful to photos.

POST-BOUND ALBUM
Type of album with two or three expandable metal posts that secure top-loading page protectors.

PRIMARY COLORS
Red, yellow and blue.

PUNCH
Small tool designed to cut a decorative shape from cardstock or paper. The resulting shape is also known as a "punch."

QUILLING
Accents comprised of thin strips of paper wound around a quilling tool, paper piercer or toothpick. Swirls are affixed next to others to form a larger shape (such as a flower) or abstract motif.

QUILTING
Creating a page background or accent that resembles a traditional quilt using trimmed pieces of cardstock.

RED-EYE PEN
Marker that removes the red glare from a subject's eyes in printed photos.

REPOSITIONABLE ADHESIVE
Type of adhesive that allows an item to be tacked down, then removed later without damage.

RESIST INK
Stamping ink designed to resist other mediums. For instance, when an image is stamped with resist ink, it will show through as a "ghosted" design when covered with dye-based ink.

REVERSE STAMPING
Process that creates a resist-like design. Ink is applied to glossy cardstock, then an un-inked stamp is pressed onto the surface, thereby lifting ink away in the form of the stamp's design.

RUB-ONS
Embellishments applied to backgrounds with a rub-on tool or Popsicle stick. Most often offered in alphabet, number, word and image styles.

RUBBER STAMP
Design cut from rubber or foam that can be inked and impressed onto paper, transferring the image.

SANDING
Distressing patterned paper, cardstock, stickers or chipboard accents by using sandpaper, steel wool or a wire brush to scratch and scrape away the top layer of color.

SCORING
Creating a thin line with a special blade or bone folder to help create a crisp fold.

SCRAPLIFT
Emulating the page design, elements or features of another scrapbooker's layout.

SECONDARY COLORS
Colors resulting from blending two primary colors.

SELF-HEALING MAT
Cutting surface used with craft knives. Can be repeatedly cut without damage.

SHADOW BOX
Case that houses and displays dimensional objects, such as memorabilia. A shadow box can be designed for layouts with mat board and a transparency window.

SHAKER BOX
Raised accent that traps tiny items like beads, confetti or punch pieces beneath a clear "window."

SHRINK PLASTIC
Plastic sheets that are stamped or written upon, then trimmed and heated to miniaturize.

SIDE-LOADING
Style of page protector that's open along one side and can be slipped over completed layouts. Designed for use with spiral-bound or strap-hinge albums.

SLIDE MOUNT
Small, plastic or cardboard frame designed to hold slides. Often used to surround small photos and accents.

SNAP
Embellishment adhered like an eyelet but without a hole in the center. Available in many colors and shapes.

SOLVENT INK
Specialty formulated, permanent stamping ink that dries quickly on slick surfaces, such as transparencies, photos, metal, glass, vellum or glossy paper.

SPIRAL-BOUND ALBUM
Album with pages secured by a metal coil running up the side.

SPONGING
Applying ink, paint or other mediums using a common kitchen, cosmetic or sea sponge.

SPRITZER
Manually operated "air gun" that forces air against the tip of a marker, creating a spatter pattern.

STAMP ALIGNER
Transparent "L"-shaped device used in conjunction with tissue paper or a transparency that allows perfect placement of stamped images.

STENCIL
Pre-cut cardboard, plastic or brass template used to trace and cut shapes.

STICKERS
Self-adhesive images, designs, borders, letters and shapes used as embellishments.

STIPPLING
Pouncing a stiff-bristled brush onto an inkpad or paint, then onto paper for a textured finish.

STITCHING
Using a traditional sewing machine or a needle and floss to add a design to cardstock. Joining two halves of a 12" x 12" layout on the computer is also known as "stitching."

STRAP-HINGE ALBUM
Album featuring pages held together with a plastic strap. Often used with side-loading page protectors.

STYLUS
A small, hand-held tool with a blunt ball tip used to trace a template to dry emboss or deboss.

SWAP
Trading supplies or completed projects with fellow scrapbookers.

T-SQUARE
Designed to draw parallel lines, this drafting tool can also be used in combination with a craft knife to make long, straight cuts.

TAGS
Whether they're purchased at the scrapbook or office supply store, tags are available in a wide range of colors, shapes and sizes.

TEMPLATE
Brass, plastic or cardboard stencil with shaped cutouts that can be used for tracing and cutting or dry embossing.

TERTIARY COLORS
Blends of primary and secondary colors, like red-orange. Also known as "intermediate colors."

THEME
The prevailing "message" or subject of a layout or specialty album.

THREE-RING ALBUM
Type of album featuring three metal rings along the spine that hold top-loading page protectors. Also known as "D-ring" albums.

TITLE PAGE
Generally the opening page of an album, designed to reveal the subjects or themes contained within.

TOP-LOADING PAGE PROTECTORS
Style of page protectors open along the top that allow layouts to be slipped inside the "pocket." Can be used with post-bound or D-ring albums.

TOTE
Bag designed especially for scrapbookers, featuring pockets and compartments to hold cardstock, tools, embellishments and other supplies.

TRANSPARENCY
Thin, clear sheet that can be stamped, etched or punched to be used as an overlay, window or background. Can withstand heat embossing or be stamped with solvent ink. Transparencies with pre-printed designs are also available.

TRIAD
Group of three colors that form a triangle on a color wheel.

VELLUM
Semi-translucent, lightweight paper that can be run through a printer, heat or dry embossed, layered, crumpled, torn and stamped. Offered in colored, printed or textured styles.

VELVETEEN PAPER
Soft specialty paper with the look and feel of velvet.

WALNUT INK
Available in crystal or liquid form, this ink created from walnut shells is used to give paper and fabrics a rich, brown stain.

WATERCOLOR PENCILS
Watercolors in pencil form that are applied like crayons but attain the appearance of watercolors when "washed" with a blender pen or wet paintbrush. Also known as "watercolor crayons."

WATERCOLORS
Transparent colorant with pigment that combines with water on paper to produce a subtle texture and wash of color.

WAX PENCIL
Soft pencils (typically in orange or black) designed to be used on photos. Also known as "grease pencils."

WORKSHOP
A class designed to teach techniques in scrapbooking, stamping, paper-crafting and journaling.

index